The Prediction Boo   ulogy

The Prediction Book of
ASTROLOGY

Peter West and Jo Logan

Blandford Press
POOLE · DORSET

First published in the U.K. 1983 by Blandford Press,
Link House, West Street, Poole, Dorset, BH15 1LL.

Copyright © 1983 Triad

Distributed in the United States by
Sterling Publishing Co., Inc.,
2 Park Avenue, New York, N.Y. 10016.

ISBN 0 7317 1243 0

All rights reserved. No part of this book may
be reproduced or transmitted in any form or by
any means, electronic or mechanical, including
photocopying, recording or any information storage
and retrieval system, without permission in
writing from the Publisher.

Typeset by Poole Typesetting (Wessex) Ltd.
Printed in Great Britain by
Butler & Tanner Ltd, Frome and London

Contents

Introduction	7
1 Erecting a Natal Chart	9
2 Time Calculations and Houses	20
3 Aspects and how to calculate them	30
4 The Planets in the Twelve Signs	35
5 The Planets in the Twelve Houses	55
6 Aspects and their significance	74
7 Signs, Parts and Special Planetary Emphasis	105
8 Assessing the Chart	115
Appendix of Tables and Data	119
Index	128

The Natural Zodiac

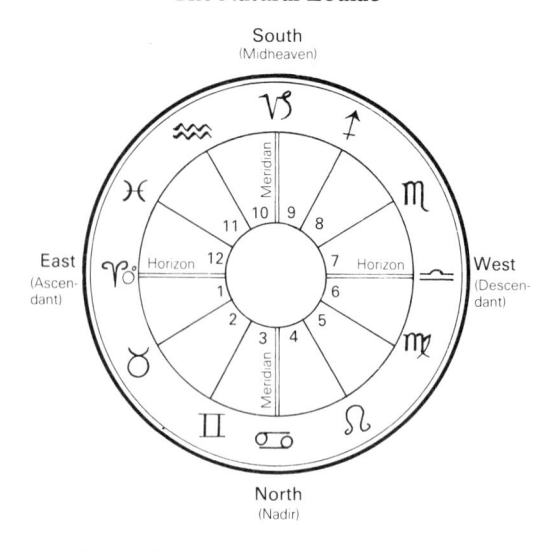

Symbols, Glyphs and Abbreviations

Aspects (Major, allow 7° Orb)			Aspects (Minor, allow 2° Orb)		
Conjunction	☌	0°	Semi-sextile	⊻	30°
Square	□	90°	Semi-square	∠	45°
Trine	△	120°	Sextile	✶	60°
Opposition	☍	180°	Quintile	Q	72°
			Sesquiquadrate	⚼	135°
			Quincunx	⚻	150°

Signs of the Zodiac

Aries	0°	♈	Libra	180°	♎
Taurus	30°	♉	Scorpio	210°	♏
Gemini	60°	♊	Sagittarius	240°	♐
Cancer	90°	♋	Capricorn	270°	♑
Leo	120°	♌	Aquarius	300°	♒
Virgo	150°	♍	Pisces	330°	♓

Planets

Sun	☉	Moon	☽
Mercury	☿	Venus	♀
Mars	♂	Jupiter	♃
Saturn	♄	Uranus	♅
Neptune	♆	Pluto	♇

Introduction

Most people are interested in astrology to some degree, even if it is simply reading their Sun sign forecasts in their daily newspapers. Yet astrology offers much more than this, for it is a very ancient art, based on the science of astronomy. Indeed, at one time astrology and astronomy were the same subject: it is only in comparatively recent times that they have diverged.

The history of astrology goes back almost as far as that of mankind. Primitive man looked to the heavens for guidance, and some of the earliest records show that the Sun, Moon and visible planets were regarded as symbols of the gods who could influence life on Earth. Each of these heavenly bodies was, therefore, awarded rulership or power over a particular sphere of human endeavour, according to the nature of the god that it symbolised. Over a period of time these associations gained credence and formed the basis of astrological theory.

Once every year the Earth makes a complete journey round the Sun, and the eight planets – Mercury, Venus, Mars, Jupiter, Saturn, Uranus, Neptune and Pluto – all revolve around the Sun in approximately the same plane as the Earth's orbit. Astrology is concerned with the relationship between the members of the Solar system and what happens on Earth, therefore the movements of the Sun, Moon and planets, as they revolve in their orbits, are calculated from a geocentric point of view: that is, as if viewed from the Earth.

The circle in which these heavenly bodies move is called the zodiac and this is divided into twelve sections known as signs. The order of these zodiacal signs is determined according to a particular sequence, starting with Aries, followed by Taurus, Gemini, Cancer, Leo, Virgo, Libra, Scorpio, Sagittarius, Capricorn, Aquarius and Pisces.

In astrological terms, the Sun is said to 'enter' each of these signs on a particular date each year and then leave it to enter the next sign on a particular date. These dates of entry can vary slightly from year to year and are listed in ephemerides – tables of planetary movements. Character analyses or forecasts based solely on the Sun's zodiacal position on the date of birth are known as Sun sign astrology and must, by definition, be somewhat limited and cannot apply, in depth, to any individual.

Natal astrology, however, where the exact time, date and location of the subject's birth are taken into consideration and an accurate birth chart drawn up, provides a much more detailed picture because all the planetary positions at the time of birth can then be calculated. In fact, the birth chart – also known as the map, natus, nativity, wheel or, more commonly, the horoscope – is the focal point of most branches of astrology.

Unfortunately, the erection and subsequent understanding of the horoscope is the biggest stumbling block with which the beginner has to contend. This, in turn, can lead to a lessening or, indeed, complete neglect of a subject that is potentially fascinating and rewarding.

For this reason, it was decided to provide a basic guide for the beginner, starting with the construction of the birth chart or map, followed by a simple explanation of how to read the erected chart. The theory and wider aspects of astrology have, therefore, been omitted in order to give as much basic instruction as possible, although it is hoped that, after reading and understanding the following chapters, the reader will follow a natural inclination to learn more.

Even if this proves not to be the case, knowing how to interpret a chart will enable you to learn much about yourself and your potential, as well as those of friends, relatives and colleagues. Natal astrology can reveal a person's temperament and the way in which he or she is likely to react to a given set of circumstances. It is fascinating to know how the other fellow ticks – why he behaves in a particular way.

Astrology can also provide a useful tool to self-knowledge because no one really sees himself as others do. So, it can be an exciting and fascinating hobby . . . you might be surprised at what you discover!

CHAPTER 1
Erecting a Natal Chart

To construct a birth chart you will need to know the time, place and date of birth of the subject.

In addition, you will require an ephemeris (astronomical tables) for the year in question. The most widely used is *Raphael's Ephemeris* which is published annually by W. Foulsham and Co. Ltd. This publication lists the longitudes of the planets; the Sidereal time for noon each day; notes the aspects; the daily motion of the planets and other phenomena, such as the Moon's phases; the time of the entry of the planets into the zodiacal signs; also the complete tables of Houses for London and Liverpool.

You will also need *Raphael's Tables of Houses for Great Britain* and *Raphael's Tables of Houses for Northern Latitudes*, as well as a good atlas with a fairly extensive gazetteer.

To complete your requirements, blank chart forms, an ordinary pocket calculator, three coloured pens, a ruler, pencil or pen and scrap paper are necessary.

You are now ready to construct your first horoscope.

Method

The completed chart overleaf is the one we are going to reconstruct. Take your time, work at your own pace, and make sure you understand each step before going on to the next. Once you have completed the work, the next chart will be considerably easier to erect, and so on. Here, then, is a step-by-step guide to erecting a natal chart.

Stage 1: calculations

1 In the top right-hand corner of the birth chart the house system employed is noted. (For the sake of simplicity, the Equal House method has been employed here although other systems are explained in chapter 2).

Noon date .... 19 .....
....

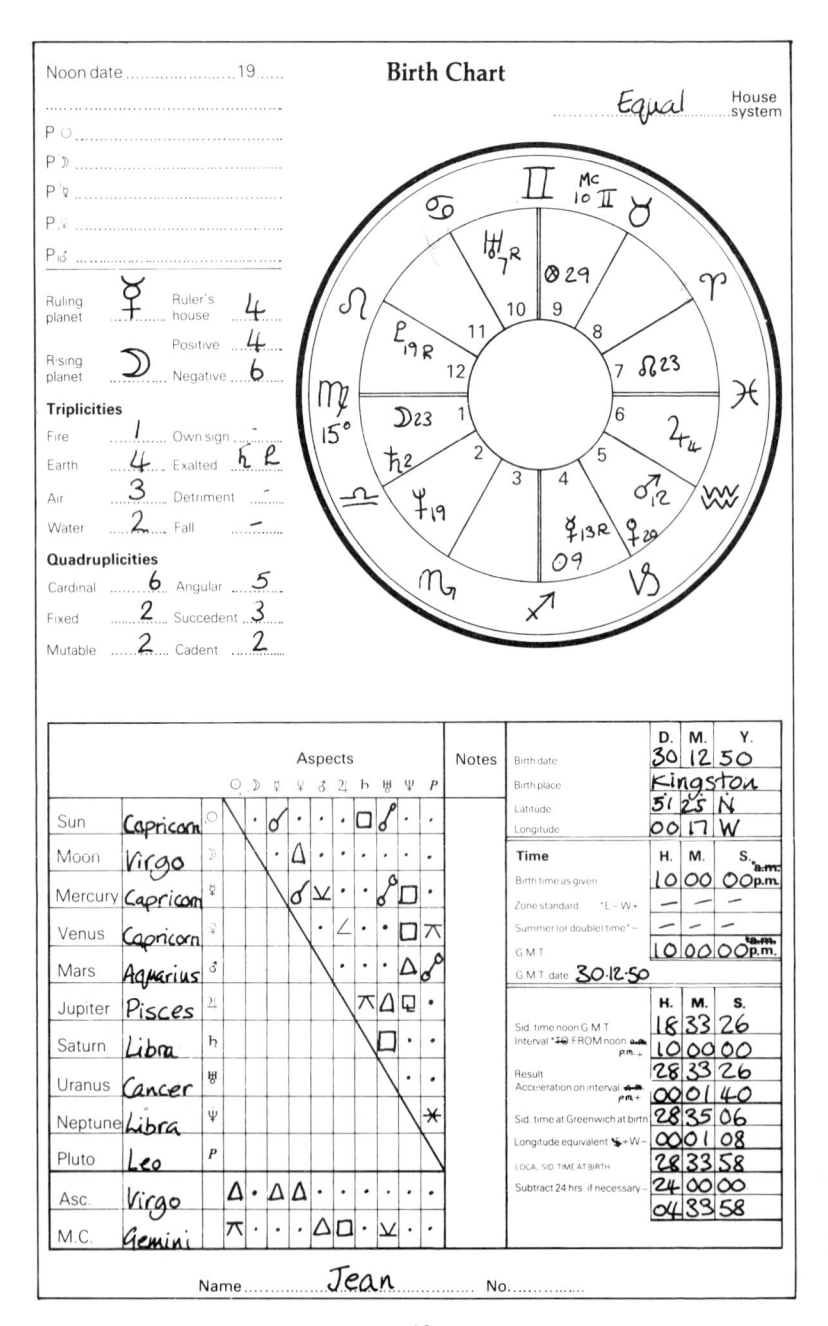

P ☉ ....
P ☽ ....
P ☿ ....
P ♀ ....
P ♂ ....

Birth Chart   Equal House system

Ruling planet	☿	Ruler's house	4
Rising planet	☽	Positive	4
		Negative	6

Triplicities
Fire .... 1 .... Own sign ....
Earth .... 4 .... Exalted ♄ ♀
Air .... 3 .... Detriment ....
Water .... 2 .... Fall ....

Quadruplicities
Cardinal .... 6 .... Angular 5
Fixed .... 2 .... Succedent 3
Mutable .... 2 .... Cadent 2

Chart positions:
MC 10 ♊
⊕ 29 (9th house)
♃ 19R ♌ (11th)
☊ 23 ♌ (8th)
♅ 7R ♋ (10th)
☽ 23 ♍ 15° (12th)
♄ 2 ♎ (1st)
♀ 19 ♎ (2nd)
♂ 12 ♒ (5th)
☿ 13R, ☉ 20 ♑ (4th)
09 (3rd)
Asc ♍, IC ♐, 6th ♓, 7th cusp

		Aspects		Notes			
		☉ ☽ ☿ ♀ ♂ ♃ ♄ ♅ ♆ ♇		Birth date	D.30	M.12	Y.50
Sun	Capricorn	☉ · ☌ · · · □ ☍ · ·		Birth place	Kingston		
				Latitude	51	25	N
Moon	Virgo	☽ · · △ · · · · · ·		Longitude	00	17	W
Mercury	Capricorn	☿ ☌ ⚹ · · ☍ □ ·		Time	H.10	M.00	S.00 p.m.
Venus	Capricorn	♀ · · ∠ · · □ ⚻		Birth time as given			
				Zone standard "E-W+"	—	—	—
Mars	Aquarius	♂ · · · △ ☍		Summer (or double) time	—	—	—
				G.M.T.	10	00	00 a.m.
Jupiter	Pisces	♃ ⚻ △ ⚼ ·		G.M.T. date 30.12.50			
Saturn	Libra	♄ □ · ·		Sid. time noon G.M.T.	H.18	M.33	S.26
				Interval TO FROM noon p.m.	10	00	00
Uranus	Cancer	♅ · · ✴		Result Acceleration on interval p.m.+	28 00	33 01	26 40
Neptune	Libra	♆ · · ✴		Sid. time at Greenwich at birth	28	35	06
Pluto	Leo	♇		Longitude equivalent E+W−	00	01	08
Asc.	Virgo	△ · △ △ · · · ·		LOCA. SID. TIME AT BIRTH	28	33	58
M.C.	Gemini	⚻ · · △ □ · ⚼ ·		Subtract 24 hrs. if necessary	24 04	00 33	00 58

Name .... Jean .... No. ....

10

2 The bottom right-hand section of the chart has to be completed to find the Ascendant, or rising sign.

3 Enter the date of birth.

4 Enter the place of birth. Make sure, though, that you check the latitude and longitude of the birth place in an atlas before entering these on the form.

5 Enter time of birth.

6 Zone standard is only used when setting up a chart for someone born abroad. (This is detailed in chapter 2).

7 Using the table of daylight saving time on *page 126*, note whether or not it is necessary to deduct one hour, or two hours if the subject was born during the war years, from the birth time in order to arrive at the GMT at birth. (It is possible that this calculation will result in the birth date having to be put back or taken forward to the day before or after the actual birth date in GMT terms. This is explained in greater detail in chapter 2.)

8 Using the ephemeris for 1950, turn to the page for December. Against the 30th you will note that the Sidereal time for noon is given as 18 hrs 33 mins 26 secs, so this should be entered into the relevant space on the birth chart, as in our sample.

9 On the next line 'a.m.' and 'to' can be deleted because our subject was born after noon, and 10 hours entered in the space provided because this represents the difference between noon and the birth time. Complete the result by adding the Sidereal time to the interval – the result will be 28 hours 33 mins 26 secs.

10 Acceleration is calculated at the rate of approximately 10 secs per hour. As 10 hours have just been added to the Sidereal time at noon it is therefore necessary to convert this interval into seconds. So, 10 × 10 secs = 100 seconds, or 1 minute 40 seconds, and enter as shown. Again, delete 'a.m.' and add this amount to the running total, which should now read 28 hrs 35 mins 06 secs.

11 It is now necessary to adjust the Sidereal time at Greenwich at birth and this is done by using the longitude of the birth place. Longitude is expressed in minutes and seconds and, if necessary, can be expressed as hours, minutes and seconds once the calculations are completed.

So, delete the 'E', because our subject was born West of Greenwich at Kingston, Surrey, which is 00°17′ W. The longitude equivalent is calculated by multiplying the longitude by four: 4 × 17 secs = 68 secs, or 1 min 8 secs, and this should be entered in the space provided. Deduct this figure from the running total and the result will read 28 hrs 33 mins 58 secs.

12 If the remaining total exceeds 24 it is necessary to deduct 24 from this figure to arrive at the local Sidereal time at birth. If, however, this total does not exceed 24, you have already calculated the local Sidereal time at birth. Our total does exceed 24 hours, so 24 is deducted from the running total and the final figure of 04 hrs 33 mins 58 secs is inserted in the space provided. (It is a good idea to do this in red so as to avoid confusion later.)

Stage 2: constructing the chart

You are now ready to construct the chart by entering the zodiacal signs and the planets on the birth chart 'wheel'. For the sake of ease and simplicity, whole degrees only will be used.

13 Turn to the *Tables of Houses, page 123,* and look at the top of each double page until you find the one which gives the longitude nearest to that of the place of birth. For our example chart, the nearest is London at 51°32' N.

Now, look down the 1st column on this page, under the heading Sidereal Time, until you find the one closest to that of our subject (remember, this was written in red at the end of the birth data calculations). In this case, the local Sidereal time at birth was 04 33 58, so the nearest figure to this is 04 33 26, and will therefore be the one we use for the next stage.

14 Next, if you look in the 4th column to the right, you will see a column headed 'Ascen' (which is short for Ascendant). Beneath this is the symbol for Virgo (♍) and, if you follow the line horizontally from the Sidereal time of 04 33 26 to this column, you will see the figure 14°45'. So, to the nearest whole degree, our subject has 15° of Virgo on the Ascendant.

15 Now, look at the wheel. At the 9 o'clock position on the outer rim (against the heavy line between 12 and 1) enter the symbol for Virgo, with the number 15 beneath it, in red. Then, in an anti-clockwise direction, complete the sequence of the twelve signs of the zodiac against each 'spoke' of the wheel. (If you are unfamilar with this sequence, the glyphs are illustrated on *page 6.*)

These spokes represent the house divisions and are known as cusps. The Ascendant sign and degree is entered in red on the 1st House cusp and every house cusp represents the same degree as that of the Ascendant because we are using the Equal House system. For instance, in the chart illustrated the 2nd House cusp will equate to 15° Libra (♎), the 3rd will be 15° Scorpio (♏) and so on.

12

16 The Midheaven (usually referred to as MC) can be found by referring back to the *Tables of Houses*. Find the Sidereal time again (04 33 26) and in the column immediately to the right which is headed '10', with the symbol for Gemini (Ⅱ) below, you will find the number 10. So, this means that our subject's MC is 10° Gemini.

17 We must now enter the MC on the chart. Remember, we are using the Equal House division system, so 15° of Gemini will already be entered on the cusp of the 9th/10th House. The zodiacal signs move continually in a clockwise direction and the first degree of Gemini would, therefore, fall halfway into the 9th House. So, the Midheaven at 10° Gemini can be entered in the outer rim of the wheel, again in red, as shown in the birth chart on *page 10*.

18 You now have the information necessary to fill in the bottom left-hand corner of the chart form. In the space provided, again in red, write Virgo against Asc. (Ascendant) and Gemini against MC (Midheaven).

Stage 3: the planetary positions

The next step is to enter the planets' positions on the birth chart wheel. Again, you will need to refer to the ephemeris for December 1950.

19 *The Sun* Each page of the ephemeris is divided horizontally by a heavy line; look down the left-hand column below this line until you find the 30th, the date of birth. Then move across to the fourth column, headed by the Sun's symbol (☉) with the word long (longitude) beneath it and you will see the figure 8°13'27". Now, move your finger up this column until you come to the glyph for one of the signs of the zodiac. In this case you will find the symbol for Capricorn (♑) on the 22nd, the date when the Sun entered that sign. So, the Sun was at 8°13'27" of Capricorn at noon on December 30, 1950, our subject's date of birth.

Next, it is necessary to calculate the Sun's position at the time of birth which, remember, was 10 hours after noon. If you look at the figure below 8°13'27" it reads 9°14'36" which means that the Sun moved 1°1'9" between noon on the 30th and noon on the 31st. You can check this out for yourself:

	degs	mins	secs
noon 31/12/50	9	14	36
minus noon 30/12/50	8	13	27
	1°	01'	09" = the movement of the Sun in 24 hours.

This final figure is the one used to find how far the Sun has moved since noon on the 30th and the birth time 10 hours later. First, we will express this figure in minutes, which gives 61 minutes if we disregard the seconds, and this is then divided by 24 and multiplied by 10. The result is 25 to the nearest minute. Thus:

	degs	mins	secs
At noon on the 30th the Sun was at	8	13	27
add 25 minutes (for 10 pm)	0	25	00
	8°	38'	27"

So, the Sun's position at the time of birth was 8°38'27" of Capricorn, or 9° Capricorn to the nearest whole degree. If you look at the birth chart you will see that the glyph for Capricorn (♑) is on the 5th House cusp at 15°. This means that the first 15° of Capricorn fall in the 4th House and the remainder are in the 5th House. If the Sun had exceeded 15° at birth it would be placed in the 5th House, but as the Sun is only at 9° Capricorn this is now written in the 4th House thus: ☉9°. Also, the word Capricorn can be entered against the Sun in the bottom left-hand corner of the chart form.

20 *The Moon* This is the fastest moving heavenly body, with an average daily motion of 13°10', though it can be as high as 15° or as low as 11°. As a very rough guide, then, the Moon moves at the rate of about ½° an hour.

Returning again to the ephemeris, in the 6th column from the left, below the heavy line, headed by the symbol for the Moon (☽) with the abbreviation for longitude beneath, is the Moon's noon position. Column 9 gives the Moon's position for midnight, 12 hours later on the same day.

The noon position for December 30 is given as 17°14'26" Virgo and the midnight position as 23°45'59" Virgo or, when reduced to whole degrees, 17° and 24° respectively. Again, we need to calculate the position for the birth time, 10 pm, which is done by dividing the Moon's movement in 12 hours (7°) by 12 and multiplying by 10 (the number of hours between noon and the birth time). The result is 6°, to the nearest whole degree, and this is added to the Moon's position at noon.

at noon	17°
add	6°
at 10 pm =	23°

The Moon's position can now be entered in the chart. Find the house with Virgo on the cusp, which is the 1st House at 15° Virgo and, as 23° is more than 15°, the Moon is placed in the 1st House thus: ☽23°. Now, write Virgo against the Moon's position in the bottom left-hand corner of the birth chart.

21 *Mercury* The position for Mercury will be found in column 8 of the ephemeris, this time on the right-hand page. This column is headed with the symbol for Mercury (☿) over the abbreviation for longitude, and at noon on December 30 this planet's position is given as 13°43' Capricorn (♑). At noon on December 31 the position is 12°27' Capricorn, less than that of the previous day.

The reason for this apparent anomaly is that, due to the motion of the planets, Mercury appeared to be travelling backward at this time. In fact, Mercury had been apparently moving backward since December 23 and, if you look at the entry for the 23rd, you will see it reads 18°10' R_e Capricorn. The symbol R_e stands for retrograde motion, and we always indicate this when entering the planet into the wheel because some astrologers are of the opinion that when a planet is retrograde its effect is lessened.

Our calculations are, therefore, slightly different this time:

Mercury's position at noon Dec 30   13° 43' Capricorn R_e
Mercury's position at noon Dec 31 *minus* 12° 27' Capricorn R_e
                                        =   1° 16'

In 24 hours Mercury has moved 1°16' and we need to know its position at 10 pm on December 30. We therefore convert this to minutes (76), divide this by 24 and multiply by 10 to arrive at 32' to the nearest minute, which represents Mercury's movement between noon and the birth time. Now we calculate Mercury's position at the time of birth.

             13° 43'
minus   32'
             13° 11' (or, to the nearest whole degree, 13° Capricorn R_e)

Capricorn is on the cusp of the 5th House at 15° and, as 13° is less than this, Mercury is entered in the 4th House thus: ☿ 15 R_e. Also, Capricorn is written against Mercury in the bottom left-hand corner of the form.

22 *Venus* Again, looking at the right-hand page of the ephemeris, the position for Venus will be found in column 7, headed by the symbol for Venus (♀) above the abbreviation for longitude.

At noon on December 30 the position is given as 19°29' Capricorn and at noon on December 31 it is 20°45' Capricorn. In 24 hours, therefore, it has moved 1°16':

             20° 45'
minus   19° 29'
              1° 16' (or 76 minutes)

To find the position of Venus at 10 pm divide 76 by 24 and multiply by 10. This results in 32', to the nearest minute, and this amount is then added to the noon position:

	19° 29'
plus	32'
	20° 01'

At 10 pm on December 30 Venus was, therefore, at 20° Capricorn (♀ 20°) and can be entered in the 5th House and in the appropriate space in the bottom left-hand corner of the form.

23 Mars The position for Mars is given in the 6th column of the right-hand page of the ephemeris under the symbol ♂ and the abbreviation for longitude. The noon position of Mars on December 30 was 11°52' Aquarius and at noon on December 31 it was 12°39'. So, in 24 hours Mars had moved 47'.

	12° 39'
minus	11° 52'
	00° 47'

The position for 10 pm is calculated by dividing 47 by 24 and multiplying by 10 and this amount – 20' to the nearest minute – is added to the noon position:

	11° 52'
plus	20'
	12° 12' (or 12° Aquarius, to the nearest whole degree)

Fifteen degrees Aquarius is on the cusp of the 6th House and 12° is less than this, so Mars and its degree value are entered in the 5th House. Continue to fill in the bottom left-hand corner of the form by writing Aquarius in the space next to Mars.

24 Jupiter The position for Jupiter will be found on the right-hand page of the ephemeris, in column 5 which is headed by the symbol for Jupiter (♃) and the abbreviation for longitude.

At noon on December 30 Jupiter's position was 4°25' Pisces and at noon on December 31 it was at 4°36'.

In 24 hours Jupiter therefore moved 11' and we require the position for 10 pm. So, divide 11 by 24, multiply by 10 and add the result (5') to 4°25', which was Jupiter's noon position:

	4° 25'
plus	05'
	4° 30'

At 10 pm on December 30 Jupiter was at 4° Pisces, to the nearest whole degree because, for ease of calculation, Jupiter's true position was previously rounded up slightly.

Fifteen degrees Pisces is on the cusp of the 7th House and, as 4° is less than this, Jupiter is placed in the 6th House (♃ 4°) and Pisces written against Jupiter in the bottom left-hand corner of the form.

25 *Saturn* On the right-hand page of the ephemeris, the position for Saturn will be found in column 4, headed with the symbol for Saturn (♄) over the abbreviation for longitude.

At noon on December 30 the position was 2°13' Libra and at noon on December 31 it was 2°15' Libra, so it only moved 2 minutes in 24 hours. It is therefore unnecessary to calculate the position at 10 pm on the 30th because it is obvious that it was 2° Libra to the nearest whole degree.

Fifteen degrees Libra is on the cusp of the 2nd House and, as 2° is less than this, Saturn is placed in the 1st House and shown thus: ♄ 2°. Continue filling in the birth chart form by writing Libra against Saturn in the bottom left-hand corner.

26 *Uranus* This planet's position will be found in the 3rd column of the right-hand page of the ephemeris below the symbol for Uranus (♅) and the abbreviation for longitude.

At noon on December 30 its position was 7°25' R_e Cancer and at noon on December 31 it was 7°22' R_e. In 24 hours Uranus only retreated 3 minutes (note the R_e sign again on December 2 where it reads 8 R_e 33 Cancer) so this need not be adjusted for the birth time.

Cancer is on the cusp of the 11th House at 15° and Uranus therefore falls in the 10th House. Enter ♅ 7° R_e in the 10th House and write Cancer against Uranus in the bottom left-hand corner of the chart.

27 *Neptune* In the ephemeris Neptune's position will be found on the right-hand page, column 2, under the symbol for Neptune (♆) and the abbreviation for longitude.

At noon on December 30 its position was 19°24' Libra and at noon on the 31st it was 19°25'. In 24 hours Neptune moved only 1 minute so there is no need to calculate the position for 10 pm because it was obviously 19° Libra to the nearest whole degree.

As 19° Libra is greater than the 15° Libra which is on the 2nd House cusp, Neptune is entered in the 2nd House as ♆ 19° and Libra written in the bottom left-hand corner of the chart next to Neptune.

28 *Pluto* Modern editions of the ephemeris list the daily positions of Pluto on the same page as the other planets. However, in the 1950 edition Pluto's position was listed separately every 10th day because it is the slowest moving of all the planets.

For the purposes of this exercise there is no need to work out the exact position for 10 pm on December 30, therefore, as this has been done for you. Pluto was at 19°30' Leo retrograde so, again using the nearest whole degree, Pluto can be entered in the chart at 19° R$_e$ Leo in the 12th House as 19° exceeds the 12th House cusp degree.

Now complete the bottom left-hand corner of the chart by putting Leo next to Pluto in the space provided.

Stage 4: Planetary data

29 To complete the information on our chart we need to fill in the section to the left-hand side of the wheel, starting with the ruling planet. Although there are occasional exceptions to the main rule, it is common practice to regard the ruling planet as that which governs the sign on the Ascendant. If you look at the table of rulerships on *page 119* you will see that Mercury rules Virgo. Therefore, Mercury is the ruling planet and its symbol (☿) is entered, as indicated, to the left of the wheel.

30 *The rising planet* is that which is closest to the Ascendant degree, irrespective of whether this planet falls in the 1st or the 12th House. Sometimes there is more than one to choose from and, in such instances, it is common practice to select the planet that is strongest by position.

Occasionally no planet can be regarded as rising because the usual practice is to designate a planet as rising only if the orb or gap between that planet and the rising degree falls within recognised limits. Some astrologers only allow 5° and others allow 10°: it is a matter of personal preference. In this chart, however, the Moon at 23° Virgo is 8° away from the Ascendant at 15° Virgo and the Moon's symbol (☽) has been entered as the rising planet.

31 *The triplicities* Despite their name, this refers to the four elements: Fire, Earth, Air and Water. Each of the zodiacal signs belongs to one of these elements and the number of planets in each of these elements is listed according to which sign they fall in. For example, if you look at the completed chart you will see that Pluto is in Leo, a Fire sign (and the only one in this example chart), so the figure 1 is entered against Fire, to the left of the birth chart wheel. (It is not unusual for there to be no planets in one or more of these elements.)

32 *The quadruplicities* This refers to the qualities credited to the zodiacal signs and these are detailed in chapter 7. These qualities are reflected by the planets that occupy those signs and are calculated in a similar way to the triplicities, and entered accordingly.

33 *Positive and negative* In astrological terms the zodiacal signs are referred to as positive or negative, masculine or feminine. Refer to the table on *page 108,* and calculate the number of positive and negative planetary positions and enter the result as shown.

34 *Own sign, exalted, detriment or fall* Calculate the positions of the planets using the rulership table on *page 119.* Some fall in their own signs, others may fall in a sign that enhances or inhibits the qualities pertaining to that planet. These positions are noted and entered as illustrated to the left of the wheel.

35 *Angular, succedent or cadent* These terms refer to the qualities allotted to the houses and are of a similar nature to the Cardinal, Fixed and Mutable signs. Usually, they are not used when employing the Equal House method of house division but they should, however, be noted for later use when interpreting the chart. Again, referring to the table on *page 108,* calculate and enter the number of planets in these categories according to their house positions.

Stage 5: completing the birth chart form

36 The data at the top left-hand corner refers to progressions and has no relevance to basic chart construction. This information can, therefore, be safely ignored at this stage but is dealt with in chapter 8.

37 *The aspect grid* and space for notes. This uncompleted section of the birth chart form may be left blank at this stage because this information is not needed for erecting basic natal charts. However, the aspect grid will have to be filled in before the chart can be interpreted properly as it is important to note the relationship of the planets to each other. Similarly, any astrological information of particular significance such as planetary patterns, Arabic parts, fixed stars, etc., should be noted in the space provided before an interpretation is attempted.

The aspects, their meanings and how to calculate them, are dealt with in chapters 3 and 6. Other astrological data will be found in chapter 7.

38 *The final check* This is probably the most important step of all, yet it cannot be done until the preceding stages have been completed: check and double check everything you have done so far. Have you written everything clearly and accurately and assigned everything to its correct position in the chart?

Do check that there are no mistakes. An error discovered now will save hours of work later.

CHAPTER 2
Time Calculations and Houses

You now have a birth chart in front of you which, except for the aspect grid and any special astrological notes that you may wish to include, is complete as far as calculations are concerned. So, what exactly has been achieved?

Well, you have erected a map of the heavens for a specific date, time and place: this is what the word horoscope means. It is a picture, or map, of the hour and is personal to the individual for whom it is erected because no one else has exactly the same natal chart (although it is theoretically possible for two people to share the same configuration, this has yet to be evidenced).

So, although our example chart is a birth chart for Jean, it also records the positions of the heavenly bodies for a specific time and geographical location. It is obviously possible, therefore, to create a map for any event, anywhere in the world, for any time and for almost any purpose.

However, our example chart has been erected for London and it is necessary to make a few adjustments when calculating a chart for elsewhere, particularly for somewhere abroad, because of the time differentials that exist between Britain and other places in the world.

Daylight Saving Time

A chart is calculated by first converting the local birth time to Greenwich Mean Time (GMT) and then making the necessary adjustments for the time and place in question. It is important, therefore, to check whether or not any daylight saving system was in operation at the time of birth.

Since 1916, many countries, including Britain, have adopted such a scheme whereby the clocks are advanced one hour at some time during the spring and the put back to 'normal' time in the autumn. However, these changes do not always take place on the same date each year or, indeed, at the same hour. These time adjustments are, therefore, very inconsistent and can lead to a great deal of confusion, particularly if one considers that in the Southern hemisphere they advance the clocks during our autumn and revert to normal time just when we officially start our Summer Time!

There are, though, publications available that list these time changes, *Time Changes in the World; Time Changes in Canada and Mexico; Time Changes in the USA* – all by Doris Chase Doane. You will need these if you want to be able to erect charts for anywhere in the world. Also, you will find a complete list of British Summer Time (BST) changes on *page 125*, including those for Double Summer Time which was in operation during some of the war years.

Time zones

The world is divided into time zones and adjustments have to be made for these, too, when calculating a chart. Any location East of the Greenwich meridian will be ahead of GMT and the time differential must therefore be subtracted at the 'zone standard' stage (step 6, chapter 1) of calculating the chart; anywhere West of Greenwich will be behind GMT and must therefore be added at this stage of the calculations.

For example, Paris uses Central European Time (CET) which is one hour in advance of GMT; New York is five hours behind and is on Eastern Standard Time (EST); and New Zealand is twelve hours ahead of Britain. So it is essential to remember to make the necessary adjustments for any difference in 'clock time' each time you prepare a horoscope.

Date changes

Occasionally time adjustments may result in the birth date as given having to be corrected, particularly if the birth time was close to midnight.

For example, the subject may say that he or she was born at 00 30 hours on June 11, 1962, quoting clock time. However, when calculating the chart one hour will have to be deducted from this because of daylight saving, thus making the real birth date June 10, 1962, with a corrected (GMT) time of 23 30 hours. Similarly, zone times may, according to where a subject was born, move the GMT date forward or backward across the midnight hour.

Whenever such date adjustments have to be made, note the new GMT date on the chart form in the space provided and continue to make your calculations using the Sidereal time for that date.

Sidereal time

Sidereal time is celestial time – time measured relative to the stars – and has no equivalent, as such, to clock time because it relates directly to the 'true' year which is not exactly 365 days but is, in fact, slightly longer. It is necessary, therefore, to record the true or Sidereal time and make an adjustment of approximately 10 seconds per hour when calculating a chart. The table on *page 127* refers to the exact amount of adjustment needed in 12 hours.

Longitude equivalent

The geographical location of the place of birth has to be expressed as time by calculating the longitude equivalent of the birth place. This is basically very simple: just multiply the longitude by 4. Thus Paris, 02°20' East, expressed as time equals 9 minutes and 20 seconds; New York, the longitude of which is 73°50' West, equals 4 hours, 55 minutes and 20 seconds. To help you convert longitude to time a table has been provided on *page 120*.

To establish the longitude of a given place, refer to the gazetteer at the back of any good atlas. Remember, when you rectify your chart calculations for the longitude equivalent (step 11, chapter 1), you must subtract for the West and add for the East.

Southern hemisphere

In effect, time is reversed south of the equator. So, if erecting a chart for the Southern hemisphere, add 12 hours to the Sidereal time before entering the Sidereal time given for noon GMT at step 8, chapter 1. Then continue to follow the steps outlined until you come to step 14, finding the Ascendant, or rising sign degree in the ephemeris. Simply 'reverse' this sign, enter it on the chart, as described in step 15, and continue filling in the rest of the chart in the normal way.

The signs of the zodiac always retain their natural order, so the same signs are always opposite one another in a chart. The natural sequence of the signs is:

Aries   is opposed by Libra
Taurus is opposed by Scorpio
Gemini is opposed by Sagittarius
Cancer is oppossed by Capricorn
Leo   is opposed by Aquarius
Virgo   is opposed by Pisces

Thus, in Jean's chart, where we calculated the Ascendant as 15° Virgo, 15° Pisces would be the rising sign degree if we reversed this for a Southern hemisphere chart.

On *page 24* is an example of the calculations for a chart for Southern latitudes. The birth data is: September 21, Palmerston North, New Zealand, at 1535 hours.

In *Raphael's Table of Houses for Northern Latitudes*, look at the tables for 40°43' North, New York, as this is the nearest equivalent to our subject's birth place which has a latitude of 40°20' South. Against the Sidereal time of 03°13'27" will be found 27° Leo rising, to the nearest whole degree. As we are dealing with a Southern latitude, we must reverse the signs: the opposite of Leo is Aquarius, so this subject's Ascendant is 27° Aquarius.

You might find it useful to keep this page open when first attempting a Southern hemisphere chart. You will then be able to check your work step by step and will be less likely to make a mistake. Once you have had a bit of practice, however, you will soon automatically make the necessary adjustments to your calculations.

House divisions

We erected the sample chart shown on *page 10* using the Equal House system, one of several methods of house division. This is the oldest system and is attributed to Ptolemy, the father of ancient astrology. The Equal House system fell into disrepute for a long time then, during the past 30-50 years or so, became widely respected again and is now employed by a large majority of astrologers who admire its ease of application.

It is not the intention to go into the deeper philosophies of differing division systems within this book because space just does not allow it. However, a brief explanation of the houses is necessary in order to understand basic astrology.

If you look at the chart we have constructed, the small circle in the centre may be regarded as representing the Earth. Looking immediately upward, the line dividing Houses 9 and 10 has 15° Gemini written at the top, signifying that at the moment of birth the constellation of Gemini appeared to be directly overhead in the sky to an observer on Earth.

To the left of the chart, at the 9 o'clock position, is 15° Virgo. So, this sign was apparently rising over the horizon at the time of birth. In the astrological sense, therefore, it is easy to see how and where all the other heavenly bodies fall into place.

	D.	M.	Y.
Birth date	21	9	1951
Birth place	Palmerston North		
Latitude	40	20	S
Longitude	175	39	E

Time	H.	M.	S.
Birth time as given	15	35	00	*a.m. p.m.
Zone standard *E– W+	12	00	00
Summer (or double) time* –	—	—	—
G.M.T.	03	35	00	*a.m. p.m.
G.M.T. date 21.9.51			

11·58·14 + 12 Hrs. for Southern latitude.	H.	M.	S.
Sid. time noon G.M.T.	23	58	14
Interval *TO/~~FROM~~ noon *a.m.– ~~p.m.+~~	08	25	00
Result	15	33	14
Acceleration on interval *a.m.– ~~p.m.+~~	00	01	23
Sid. time at Greenwich at birth	15	31	51
Longitude equivalent *E+ ~~W–~~	11	42	36
LOCAL SID. TIME AT BIRTH	27	14	27
Subtract 24 hrs. if necessary –	24	00	00
Reverse signs for Southern Latitude.	03	14	27

Calculations for a chart for Southern Latitudes

All this information is published in advance annually in *Raphael's Astronomical Ephemeris of the Planets' Places*, with tables of houses for London, Liverpool and New York, and in *Raphael's Tables of Houses for Northern Latitudes*. These tables are, in fact, for the Placidus House division system which is, perhaps for this reason, the second most popular in use today.

However, this system can present certain problems for the student because, the further north the place of birth, the more disproportionate the Placidus House divisions become. This may result in one or more of the signs being 'intercepted' which is very confusing for the beginner.

The Equal House system simply divides the ecliptic, or path of the Sun, into 30° arcs from the Ascendant so that each house comprises 30° and each house cusp represents the same degree as that of the Ascendant. The Placidus system, however, involves intercepting the diurnal circle and, as some signs are of longer ascension than others, this results in unequal house divisions and differing cusp degrees.

Also, it is necessary to use logarithms (or a slide-rule) to calculate a chart by the Placidus method, so it is perhaps simpler for a beginner to use the Equal House system until he or she feels confident enough to experiment with other systems and then choose the one with which he feels happiest. There are, in fact, several alternative systems to choose from: Porphyry, Regiomontanus, Alcabitius, Campanus, Morinus, Zariel and Koch (this latter is favoured by some American astrologers) and standard astrological reference books will provide details of the various systems.

Yet, whichever system is employed, the significance of the houses remains constant: each house relates to a specific area of the subject's life and his attitude towards this will reflect the nature of the planet (or planets) that occupies the house in question as well as the sign on the cusp of that house.

The houses

Traditionally, a house was regarded as the 'place' of a planet and related to the sign that was ruled by that planet. Thus there is a dual correspondence between the houses, signs and planets. For example, Jupiter rules Sagittarius and is therefore regarded as being powerfully placed (i.e. its influence will be emphasised) when it occupies the 9th House because this house corresponds to Sagittarius in the natural order of the zodiac. In other words, the 9th House is the 'natural' house of Sagittarius, the ninth sign of the zodiac. In the same way, the 1st House corresponds to Aries, the first sign of the zodiac, although this sign may not, of course, actually be on the cusp of the 1st House in a chart drawn up for a particular person or event.

As the Earth rotates on its axis each day the signs move through the houses, some slightly faster than others, so that at any given moment a specific part (i.e. degree) of one of these signs will be on the 1st House cusp. So, when we erect a chart we note what degree of which sign is at this point, and call this the Ascendant.

The Ascendant, rising sign or 1st House cusp, is regarded as very important by most astrologers. The planet that rules this sign is said to rule the chart, which is why we list this information on the left-hand side of the chart wheel along with the position of the planet. Indeed, some astrologers credit the chart ruler with such importance that some reference works devote a whole chapter to listing its meaning or significance in the various houses.

As stated previously, each house relates to specific areas of the subject's life and planets and signs fall within a house's sphere of activity, according to their position in a chart. The meanings allocated to the houses are based partly on the traditional correspondences and partly on the research and experience of modern astrologers. Also, by polarity, the first six houses correlate with the second six: there are 'links' between the 1st and 7th Houses, the 2nd and 8th, and so on.

1st House
This relates to the subject's personality: the image he or she presents to the world. It denotes the person's temperament, disposition, physical appearance and has a bearing on his manner and approach to others.

The sign ruling the cusp and any planet that occupies the 1st House will, therefore, have a strong influence on the individual's vitality and behavioural patterns, as will any planet conjunct the Ascendant.

2nd House
This house represents money and worldly goods. It relates to material possessions (movable goods as opposed to real estate), income and expenditure, financial resources and the subject's attitude towards these areas of his life.

It also refers to feelings and emotions, as well as the necessities of life. The nature of the planets that occupy this house and the sign on the cusp will indicate the native's manner of meeting obligations.

3rd House
This house denotes the subject's immediate environment: his normal, day-to-day contacts and associates such as brothers, sisters, neighbours or schoolfriends. It therefore relates to the individual's routine interactions with others.

The 'natural' house of Gemini, it is also concerned with communication, education, languages, written agreements, short journeys – especially by road and rail – and the subject's mental attitude.

4th House
This house signifies the home as a base: the subject's personal, private life, both as a child and as an adult. It relates to his roots – parents, forebears and native land – and denotes his attitude to the past and traditional concepts or, in other words, his sense of belonging.

It also refers to real estate, the place of residence, living conditions, patriotism and physical strength as well as the end and beginning of life.

5th House
This is the house of creativity, of self-expression, and relates to offspring, pleasures and amusements, courtship, sex and pregnancy, gambling and speculation.

It also refers to enterprises and new undertakings; to objects of instinctive affection such as pets, playmates and sweethearts. Leisure – holidays, the theatre, entertainment – is also concerned with this house, as are colleagues, teachers and instructors.

6th House
This house rules work, health and service to others. It relates to the individual's employment and attitude to subordinates, superiors and work colleagues.

An abundance of planets in this house may denote that the subject's work figures largely in his life and occupies much of his time. Alternatively, such a planetary emphasis could indicate his great concern with health, hygiene and related matters.

7th House
This is the house of partnerships, whether business or personal. It relates to love, marriage, spouse and close relationships (but not relatives). Traditionally, it is also the house of open enemies and refers to litigation, law suits, contracts and the like.

Accordingly, planets here will indicate the subject's attitude to his peers and his dealings with associates, business colleagues or rivals, opponents, adversaries or competitors; the sign on the cusp may signify the partner.

8th House
This house signifies death, wills, legacies and other people's money. It relates to the individual's financial ability and the marriage partner's

estate. It also refers to big business such as the stock market, banking and insurance.

It is the house of transformation and spiritual regeneration and therefore concerns sex, birth, death, rebirth, the occult and the subject's attitude to such matters.

9th House
This house denotes the higher mind, religion, philosophy, the law, long journeys and sea voyages. It relates to further education, places of learning, courts of law, the Church, morals, conscience, visions and dreams, also foreign people and places.

A planetary emphasis on this house will indicate the subject's attitude towards the confines of his everyday world. His acceptance or otherwise of the limitations – both geographically and metaphysically – will depend on the planets involved.

10th House
This house is concerned with external aspects of life: career, status, ambitions. It relates to the native's reputation, social and public standing, professional ambitions and achievements, responsibilities and so on.

The individual's attitude to these matters and people in authority – employers, officials, the government, royalty – will reflect the nature of the planet or planets in this house.

11th House
This is the house of friends, acquaintances, clubs and societies. It relates to all group activities and the more detached contacts of day-to-day life. Intellectual, as opposed to physical pleasures, sports or pastimes also come under the auspices of this house.

An abundance of planets here would emphasise social relationships and, depending on the planets concerned, indicate the subject's likely aspirations.

12th House
Traditionally, this house is known as the house of one's self-undoing and corresponds to the inner, more secretive aspects of life: fantasies, daydreams, conspiracies, intrigues and secret enemies.

It relates to places of seclusion or restraint – hospitals, prisons, asylums, orphanages and so on – and the nature of any inhibiting elements or karmic responsibilities in the subject's life will be indicated by the planets occupying this house.

These, then, are the basic meanings of the twelve houses: the areas of life that correspond to each of the houses. However, as stated previously, the houses, planets and signs correlate, so here is a list of the planets (in their normal sequence as listed on a chart form) and their associated keywords to help you understand their astrological function:

Sun – Vitality, creativity, power.
Moon – Emotion, response, sensitivity.
Mercury – Communication, perception, expression.
Venus – Harmony, love and affection, companionship.
Mars – Energy, assertiveness, construction, courage.
Jupiter – Expansion, optimism, maturity.
Saturn – Responsibility, limitation, stability.
Uranus – Change, progression, freedom.
Neptune – Intuition, imagination, illusion, idealism.
Pluto – Regeneration, transformation, intensity, elimination.

N.B. In astrological terms the Sun and Moon are regarded as planets although they are sometimes referred to as lights or luminaries.

Later chapters (4 and 5) define the way in which the planetary influences will manifest according to the signs and houses that they occupy.

CHAPTER 3
Aspects and how to calculate them

In astrology, the term 'aspect' refers to an angular distance between two points, as measured along the ecliptic.

The ecliptic, or path of the Sun, is equal to 360° – the measurement of a circle, which is what a birth chart represents. From 0° Aries to the 30th degree of Pisces is 360°. At any time, two or more planets may form recognised aspects to each other or to parts of the chart that are considered important: the Ascendant, the Midheaven or the house cusps.

There are four major aspects: conjunction, opposition, trine and square. There are six minor aspects: semi-sextile, semi-square, sextile, quintile, sesquiquadrate and inconjunct or quincunx.

There are many others; some are old and have fallen into disuse, some are new but are not used by all astrologers. For our purposes, though, we will concentrate on those mentioned and give an indication of their significance in a birth chart.

The major aspects

☌ *The conjunction – focalising energy*   ☌

When two planets occupy the same space or degree, or when they are approaching or separating from each other within a reasonably close orb, this is called a conjunction. Although different astrologers allow different degrees of orb for a conjunction, the distance between the two relevant planets must be small in order for them to be regarded as conjunct.

For example, if the Sun is at 5° Aries and Mars is at 5° Aries, this is an exact conjunction. However, if the Sun were at 5° Aries and Mars at 10° Aries, they would still be in a conjunct position. Similarly, if the Sun were 5° Aries and Mars at 28° Pisces, this would also be considered as a conjunction. Some astrologers allow an orb of up to 15° for the luminaries – the Sun and the Moon – and as little as 5° for the other planets. For simplicity, therefore, an orb allowance of 7° is recommended for a conjunction as a general rule.

However, it is important to note whether the aspect is applying (the planets concerned are moving closer together) or separating (moving further apart) in order to assess the value of your interpretation of the aspect. For example, if the Sun is at 5° Aries and Pluto at 10° Aries, the Sun – which is the faster moving body – would be applying to Pluto because this is the slowest moving of all the planets. Your interpretation would, therefore, have to allow for the fact that the Sun was moving towards Pluto, or applying closer. But, should Pluto be at 10° Aries and the Sun at 15° Aries, then the aspect would be a separating conjunction because the Sun would be moving away from the other planet.

If you remember this simple rule you will learn to recognise the value of an aspect when it is beyond the recommended orb of 7°. A little common sense and judgement are required. Do not take the attitude that the meaning of a particular aspect is always 'such and such': experiment, learn to make judgements of your own based on the guidelines given.

☍ *The opposition – conflict and tension*
An opposition occurs when two or more planets literally oppose one another in the chart. A planet at 15° Cancer, for instance, will be in opposition to another at 15° Capricorn or, for that matter, to any planet that falls within the range 8°-22° Capricorn. Again, an allowance of 7° is recommended. Note, too, whether it is a separating or applying aspect: decide which is the faster moving planet and consider whether the orb is widening or closing.

□ *The square – mostly challenging*
A square aspect occurs when two or more planets are 90° apart. Using the same rule as before – allowing an orb of 7° – this means that a planet at 1° Aries will be in square aspect to another planet at 1° Cancer or to one at 1° Capricorn.

△ *The trine – strongly helpful*
A trine aspect is one where the planets are 120° apart. Again, the same rules apply and the recommended orb is 7°. So, a planet at 1° Aries will be in trine aspect to another planet at 1° Leo or 1° Sagittarius.

The minor aspects

⚺ *The semi-sextile – slightly favourable*
The semi-sextile occurs when two or more planets are 30°, or one sign

apart. The suggested orb of influence is 2° and it is recommended that anything greater than this should be discounted.

∠ *The semi-square – a little stressful*   45
The semi-square is 45°, or one and a half signs apart. Again, the suggested allowable orb is 2°.

⁎ *The sextile – generally helpful*   60
The sextile is 60°, or two signs apart. As before, a 2° orb is all that should be allowed for this aspect.

Q *The quintile – creativity*   72
The quintile occurs when planets are 72° apart, or one fifth of the circle. Again, the orb should not be wider than 2°.

⌑ *The sesqui-square – unfavourable*   135
The sesqui-square is 135°, or four and a half signs apart. Although this aspect is little used, a maximum 2° orb is recommended.

⚻ *The quincunx – stressful*   150
The inconjunct, or quincunx aspect is 150°, or five signs apart. In the last few years or so this aspect has become more widely used by astrologers. Not more than 2° should be allowed for the orb.

Calculating the aspects

This is simply a succession of small sums – additions and/or subtractions – and, when using the Equal House method, is very easy to do.

If you look at the aspect grid on the sample birth chart in chapter 1, *page 10*, you will see that the symbols for the planets are listed downwards from the Sun through to Pluto on the left-hand side. Along the top of the grid is the same list of planets and a thick diagonal line which runs from the top left to the bottom right-hand corner indicates where to start marking in the aspects.

Using this sample chart for guidance, we will now calculate what aspects are made between the planets, step by step.

Step 1:
First, we will consider any aspects made to the Sun. On a separate sheet of paper, write in the zodiacal longitude of the planet as a number. In this case, the Sun is at 9° Capricorn. Remember, there are 360° in the zodiacal circle and this is divided into 12 equal sections, so each sign

32

consists of 30°, starting with 0° Aries. Capricorn is the 9th sign of the zodiac, or 270° from 0° Aries; so 270°+9° = 279° or just 279.

Step 2:
Determine the position of the next listed planet, the Moon. This is located at 23° Virgo (the 5th sign): 150°+23° = 173°, or just 173. As 279 is greater than 173, deduct the latter from the former to arrive at the distance between these two planets in zodiacal longitude; 279−173 = 106 which, if you check with the measurements given, is not a recognised aspect degree. It is 16 away from 90 – the square – or 14 away from 120 – the trine – so, for our purposes, there is no aspect between the Sun and the Moon because they do not fall within the allowable orbs.

Put a dot in the centre of the relevant square on the aspect grid to indicate that this calculation has been made but that there is no aspect to be entered. It is advisable to enter the relevant symbol for each aspect found, or just a dot to indicate that the calculation has been made each time in order to insure that you do not miss a calculation and to remind you how far you have progressed if you are interrupted in your work.

Step 3:
The next listed planet, Mercury, is situated at 13° retrograde of Capricorn, or 283° from 0° Aries. The Sun is at 279 so: 283−279 = 4. This is within the 7° orb allowance for a conjunction. The Sun is therefore conjunct Mercury and the symbol for a conjunction is entered into the aspect grid as illustrated.

Step 4:
Continue to check each planet's position in relation to the Sun until you reach Pluto. When you have finished the Sun line on the aspect grid you will have found two more aspects: Sun square Saturn (97 apart) and Sun opposition Uranus (182 apart).

Step 5:
Calculate the aspects made to the Moon, enter the results and compare your findings with the completed aspect grid shown. You should only have one, a trine to Venus. The Moon is at 23° Virgo, or 173°, and Venus is at 20° Capricorn, or 290°, so the difference is 117 which falls within a 3° orb to the trine.

Step 6:
Continue to calculate the rest of the aspects in a similar manner and compare your findings with the illustration on *page 10*.

Step 7:
Aspects to the Ascendant and the Midheaven (MC) are calculated in exactly the same way, except that a slightly wider orb may be allowed, perhaps a degree or two if there is an important planetary position to record.

For example, in our chart, Uranus at 7° retrograde of Cancer is 27° from the Midheaven of 10° Gemini, or 3° away from an exact semi-sextile. So, this has been entered as a semi-sextile in our example chart where we have only entered the major and minor aspects for guidance.

Step 8:
Aspects that are exact are often marked with a tiny letter E in the corner of the relevant square on the aspect grid. This serves a useful purpose because it emphasises the aspect, not only for interpretative purposes but also for making an assessment of the whole view at a later date *(see chapter 8)*.

Other considerations

From time to time an aspect occurs when one planet is at the end of a sign and the other planet is in the beginning of the next sign. This is called a disassociated aspect and its effect is considered to be weakened.

When two planets in aspect each occupy the sign ruled by the other – Venus in Aries, in opposition to Mars in Libra, for example – the general effect will be to emphasise the power of that aspect. In the example quoted, for instance, the aspect made – an opposition – may be regarded as being strengthened by the power of a conjunction as well. Not all astrologers favour this view but it should, perhaps, be borne in mind.

There are other aspects to be taken into account where patterns are made by three, four or more planets. Such configurations are explained in the chapter on special planetary emphasis, chapter 7. The significance of the major aspects in a natal chart is outlined in chapter 6.

CHAPTER 4
The Planets in the Twelve Signs

A brief summary of the significance of each planet in each sign.

(1) The Sun

☉ in ♈ *Sun in Aries*
Creative energy, enthusiasm and initiative are the qualities associated with the first sign of the zodiac. Aries subjects are highly competitive and make good leaders although they may lack tact and diplomacy when seeking to achieve an aim for they can be extremely selfish. They can be impatient, overbearing and arrogant but, more positively, they can also be brave, quick-witted and adventurous. They need to learn to relate to others and to think a little more about the needs of those around them.

☉ in ♉ *Sun in Taurus*
Determined and stubborn, practical and reliable, Taureans are very security-conscious. Usually, they possess good business abilities and will utilise these in order to obtain those material possessions which mean a lot to them. They have powerful emotions and are quite sensitive, although they can lack flexibility. Patient, trustworthy and loyal, they are reluctant to take risks, even when it is necessary. They tend to be somewhat self-indulgent and may have a lazy streak, yet they will pursue their goals with dogged determination.

☉ in ♊ *Sun in Gemini*
Adaptable, versatile and clever, Geminians need to be constantly on the go, both mentally and physically, and tend to live on nervous energy. Changeable, restless and inconsistent, they find it difficult to concentrate on any one issue for very long and, due to their insatiable curiosity, tend to acquire a superficial knowledge of numerous subjects. They revel in the art of communication, in every sense, and are always popular because of their ease of sociability and courteous manner.

Slightly unconventional, Geminians are the eternal children of the zodiac.

☉ in ♋ *Sun in Cancer*
Complex and diplomatic, Cancerians possess a built-in defensive mechanism which few, if any, will penetrate and understand. Highly sensitive and deeply emotional, they are kind and sympathetic yet may be quite unforgiving because they can never forget a slight. Tenacious when pursuing their aims, they tend to cling to old ideas and possessions for far too long. They have powerful imaginations and are not adverse to using people, often quite dispassionately, yet they make the most loyal of friends and are excellent parents and home-makers.

☉ in ♌ *Sun in Leo*
To function properly Leos need to be the centre of attraction. Broad-minded, expansive and self-confident, they are also enthusiastic and domineering. They usually possess a keen sense of drama which, when combined with natural inspiration, gives them an unassailable aura of authority. However, they can become quite patronising, conceited, intolerant and snobbish because, to them, the end justifies the means and they will pursue an ambition or goal irrespective of the disapproval of others.

☉ in ♍ *Sun in Virgo*
Whatever they do Virgoans have an eye for detail – they will either prove to be meticulous or downright finicky. Emotionally reserved, they worry unnecessarily over trivia and the larger issues tend to pass by unnoticed. They can be highly-strung and inhibited and may find it difficult to relax or to relate to others in a balanced way due to their natural reticence. Virgo, without doubt, is the sign of service and these subjects really do function best when doing something useful, preferably for others.

☉ in ♎ *Sun in Libra*
Librans need the company of others in order to shine and they function best in partnerships. However, curiously enough, they do need occasional solitude despite their constant need for physical and mental stimulation. The are concerned with society and its make-up, especially human relationships, and have a strong sense of fair play although they will bend the rules to suit their own ends. Librans can also be indecisive, changeable and too easily influenced. However, once a decision has been made they will generally stick to it.

☉ in ♏ *Sun in Scorpio*
Powerful emotions dominate Scorpio subjects, whatever their activities. They always have a sense of purpose and can be determined and

persistent although they can also be resentful, jealous, obstinate, intractable, secretive and not always tactful. Usually physically robust, they may have a tendency to hypochondria, despite their tremendous staying power and ability to fight off all opposition. Their magnetic personalities, coupled with natural intuition, ensure their survival – everything and everyone will be sacrificed if necessary in order to come out on top.

○ in ♐ *Sun in Sagittarius*
Honest and straightforward, energetic and outgoing, Sagittarians love freedom and liberty. Idealistic and scrupulously fair, they can be irresponsibly boisterous, careless and capricious. They tend to jump to conclusions easily but do not always see the wood for the trees. They love tradition yet also like the new and untried; they like flattery but can spot the con artist a mile away. More often than not, Sagittarians become pillars of society when they reach middle age although they never really lose their somewhat childlike innocence and sense of humour.

○ in ♑ *Sun in Capricorn*
Reliable, determined, prudent and cautious, Capricornians are very practical and have an inborn sense of discipline. Neat and methodical, with a capacity for hard work, they have great faith in their own power and ability: they will not seek favours, nor will they give them. They can be too conventional, too rigid, unforgiving and mean. Their relationships may prove difficult because they have a tendency to be loners although they are warm and loving to those they choose as friends. They tend to worry too much about material status but have a delightfully dry sense of humour.

○ in ♒ *Sun in Aquarius*
Friendly, independent, willing and inventive, Aquarians are often quite unpredictable and can be extremely stubborn. They are humanitarian, warm and loving, but beneath that calm exterior lurks a seething mass of worry, indecision and anxiety which often leads to some form of eccentric behaviour. Natural rebels, Aquarians care little for the thoughts and opinions of others and need to exercise their intellect in jobs that are not too routine.

○ in ♓ *Sun in Pisces*
Sensitive, sympathetic, impressionable, warm and loving, Pisceans seek quiet lives with as little trouble as possible. They are torn by their emotions, always desperate to do the right thing, and need to learn to stand on their own two feet. They can be weak-willed, easily confused and influenced, and tend to live in worlds of their own making. Yet they

are true romantics and have the highest ideals. These gentle dreamers, so intuitive and sentimental, need to become firmer, more practical and resolute.

(2) The Moon

☽ in ♈ *Moon in Aries*
Emotionally volatile and quick-tempered, these subjects are inclined to lust for power and their precipitate actions often cause problems. Such folk are usually quite independent although they may tend to take the reactions of others personally.

☽ in ♉ *Moon in Taurus*
Financial security and material possessions are absolutely necessary for this individual's emotional happiness. In general, these individuals are resolute in the pursuit of their material comforts although they may display changeable attitudes in other areas of their lives.

☽ in ♊ *Moon in Gemini*
Changeable, quick-witted and resourceful, these subjects tend to spread themselves too thinly and have too many irons in the fire at once. Avid students, restless and easily bored, they are, literally, jacks of all trades and rarely master of anything.

☽ in ♋ *Moon in Cancer*
Emotional intensity, sensitivity and moodiness are the keynotes. Such people are affectionate and impressionable but may appear withdrawn. The Moon here emphasises domestic issues, and these subjects often make good parents although discipline could present a problem.

☽ in ♌ *Moon in Leo*
Proud, dramatic and self-centred, these subject love luxury, are somewhat self-indulgent and inclined to be stubborn. The home is often a focal point of their lives although good creative talents and organising ability often lead to careers that deal directly with the public.

☽ in ♍ *Moon in Virgo*
This signifies a good business head, an eye for detail, but an over-anxious personality. Such folk may be shy and retiring. Practical and methodical, they often make good cooks because of their interest in dietary matters and genuine concern for health and hygiene.

☽ in ♎ *Moon in Libra*
Personal charm and courtesy mark these subjects who, nevertheless, can be self-indulgent and easily side-tracked despite their obvious

sociability. They may dislike making and abiding by decisions and usually function best in partnerships because they rely on the approbation of others.

☽ in ♏ *Moon in Scorpio*
Intense and possessive, these people are highly emotional. Often very stubborn, self-discipline can present a problem and, although they may work hard, they will play hard, too. Usually, they keep their personal affairs secret and may, therefore, appear to be a little hypocritical.

☽ in ♐ *Moon in Sagittarius*
Restless, optimistic and cheerful, such individuals are studious and fond of travel. Sometimes too idealistic, they can appear to be narrow-minded and very prudish as they have difficulty in expressing views without being subjective. Fond of exercise, these folk are often attracted to sports, particularly in youth.

☽ in ♑ *Moon in Capricorn*
A repressed emotional life can cause these people to become withdrawn and they may appear cold. Hard-working, ambitious and very status conscious, they seek security through material possessions and can be very calculating. They may appear old before their time – an old head on a young body.

☽ in ♒ *Moon in Aquarius*
Independent, humane, sympathetic and intuitive, these subjects are reluctant to become too deeply involved emotionally in case their personal freedom is threatened. Original and inventive, they are very changeable – even erratic and eccentric – and often suffer from nervous tension.

☽ in ♓ *Moon in Pisces*
Receptive, super-sensitive and very idealistic, such folk are extremely impressionable and sometimes have mediumistic or psychic abilities. Easily hurt and discouraged, psychological problems can arise if these subjects fail to control their over-active imaginations.

---

(3) **Mercury**

☿ in ♈ *Mercury in Aries*
Decisive and competitive, these subjects are able both to originate ideas and put them to practical use. Often impulsive and hasty, they dislike opposition and delays, and are inclined to be outspoken. Concerned with creating an impression, they may sometimes act at the last moment in order to be seen acting constructively.

☿ in ♉ *Mercury in Taurus*
Practical, steady and patient, such folk may be inflexible in their views. They possess good powers of concentration and plenty of common sense and therefore make reliable friends and employees. Cheerful, with a good clean sense of fun, they like routine and dislike having their lives disrupted in any way.

☿ in ♊ *Mercury in Gemini*
Mercury in Gemini indicates good reasoning powers, often combined with intense curiosity. These individuals possess eloquence, are well-read and knowledgeable, although this may only be superficial in some subjects. They may appear to lack emotional warmth because of their apparent fickleness. Very changeable and mentally active, they often have several things on the go at any one time.

☿ in ♋ *Mercury in Cancer*
A good memory is indicated and this is often accompanied by an equally keen imagination. Such people are perceptive and find it easy to learn, but only those things that most interest them. It is easy to appeal to their intense emotions although these subjects often agree to take on more than they can reasonably handle.

☿ in ♌ *Mercury in Leo*
Strong will-power combined with an unswerving sense of purpose may make these subjects a trifle arrogant and forceful. They plan well because they find it easy to concentrate for long periods at a time, but have a tendency to overlook details in favour of the larger issues. Usually, such folk have a marked executive ability and make good managers.

☿ in ♍ *Mercury in Virgo*
This individual may be shy and retiring, interested only in practical matters that require precision, logic or specialised skills. Health, diet and hygiene will be important to this person who may be over-fussy and over-tidy. Versatile and intelligent, such an individual may exhibit scepticism although he or she usually works well as part of a team.

☿ in ♎ *Mercury in Libra*
Peace and harmony are essential to this subject who needs to associate with those having the same degree of personal discipline. Creative, artistic and intellectual, such an individual has a strong sense of justice and fair play. Sometimes slow to make decisions, this person will prove intractable in the face of opposition if he feels he is in the right.

☿ in ♏ *Mercury in Scorpio*
Intuitive, perceptive and critical, these folk have sharp tongues. They revel in behind the scenes activity and love delving into mysteries. By

nature strongly investigative, they often possess an uncanny insight into the heart of a problem and can offer practical solutions after suitable deliberations.

☿ in ♐ *Mercury in Sagittarius*
Sincere and versatile, humanitarian issues preoccupy these subjects who possess a strong social sense. Somewhat traditional in outlook, these folk can become too set in their beliefs and ideals; this may cause inner conflict if their natural sense of right and wrong is challenged.

☿ in ♑ *Mercury in Capricorn*
Methodical and conservative, these folk are ambitious and shrewd. They can, however, be narrow-minded and lack humour, often with a stick-in-the-mud attitude. Concerned with material status, they are realists and are seldom taken in by false idealism.

☿ in ♒ *Mercury in Aquarius*
Unemotional and impersonal but with strong humanitarian instincts, these people possess a good insight into the motivations of those around them. Although they are realists at heart, they are prepared to try anything new that catches their attention; quite often the occult, particularly astrology, provides a mental outlet for them.

☿ in ♓ *Mercury in Pisces*
Somewhat over-sensitive and intuitive, these individuals are frequently very artistic. A trifle secretive, they tend to daydream their lives away, missing opportunities when they do occur. Many such subjects are talented entertainers, usually in one of the higher art forms.

(4) Venus

♀ in ♈ *Venus in Aries*
This indicates an impulsive, emotional outlook – ardent and romantic. These subjects are extroverts and have likeable personalities, although they can be coarse and sometimes act like spoilt children. They need to exercise special care in financial dealings and should not enter into any form of business speculation.

♀ in ♉ *Venus in Taurus*
Over-possessive emotionally, these people can be constant and faithful – while the attraction lasts. Their appearance may be refined, their behaviour loyal and upright, yet underneath they tend to be passionate and sensual. They love luxury, have extravagant tastes, and often take up agricultural pursuits, the arts or entertainment, especially music.

♀ in ♊ Venus in Gemini
These folk need constant variety in both their business and social lives in order to achieve complete satisfaction. Charming, courteous and very sociable, they tend to have a somewhat superficial attitude towards romance and money simply goes through their hands like water.

♀ in ♋ Venus in Cancer
Easily hurt and prone to moodiness, these individuals need strong partners who can understand and cope with their unpredictability. Romantically they are deeply sensitive; their domestic environment needs to be comfortable and will often form the base for entering potential partners.

♀ in ♌ Venus in Leo
Affectionate, cheerful warm-hearted and thoroughly outgoing, these subjects naturally gravitate towards the opposite sex because they love their company. Marriage comes easily to such folk, usually early in life. Often rather theatrical, they love acting and this is sometimes taken up as a career.

♀ in ♍ Venus in Virgo
These folk are well liked and often pursue careers that involve helping others. They can be critical, yet they like to share their lives as fully as possible with their partners and can be deeply passionate, despite outer appearances. Incorrect or coarse behaviour is definitely unacceptable to such subjects.

♀ in ♎ Venus in Libra
These subjects have a constant desire to please and to be pleased and enjoy their creature comforts. They find any form of discord abhorrent and will go to great lengths to avoid trouble. Well suited for public life, they often make careers in politics or the performing arts.

♀ in ♏ Venus in Scorpio
Emotional intensity can often be the undoing of these folk because their strong passions are only just below the surface at all times. Self-indulgence and too much idealism may result in negative behaviour. They tend to have few close friends due to a lack of reasonableness and tact, but usually enjoy a wide circle of acquaintances.

♀ in ♐ Venus in Sagittarius
These individuals usually appear cold and undemonstrative until one gets to know them properly, which is not always easy. They love freedom and independence, sometimes at the cost of friendship, career or even marriage. Traditionalists at heart, they often follow classical studies, either as a career or as a hobby.

♀ in ♑ *Venus in Capricorn*
The qualities of pride and reserve can present difficulties for these subjects as they dislike showing their real feelings, except to those very close to them. Loyal, hard-working and persevering, they seek status through wealth and possessions, sometimes marrying 'above their station' to achieve this aim.

♀ in ♒ *Venus in Aquarius*
Impersonal but with a friendly manner, these people have a strong love of freedom, especially in romantic affairs. Slightly rebellious, they tend to live by their own rules and may develop an eccentric mode of dress – for the sheer pleasure of shocking others.

♀ in ♓ *Venus in Pisces*
Romantic, sensitive and idealistic, these folk have great compassion and sympathy for others, no matter who they are. Often artistically gifted, their talents are largely inspirational. However, these individuals tend to lack drive and therefore need strong partners on whom they can rely.

(5) Mars

♂ in ♈ *Mars in Aries*
Headstrong and independent, these subjects possess the energy, initiative and enthusiasm necessary to create new enterprises and projects. Sport attracts such folk, especially mechanically orientated pursuits such as motor-racing. They are natural leaders and organisers but need to develop persistence in order to complete their undertakings.

♂ in ♉ *Mars in Taurus*
Practical and clever, acquisitive and possessive, these people may lack tact and diplomacy. Although imaginatively limited, slow to perceive and begin projects and schemes, they do possess the perseverance and determination to see things through to the bitter end. They may be highly sexed and are inclined to be possessive and jealous.

♂ in ♊ *Mars in Gemini*
Restless, mentally alert, inclined to be talkative, such folk lack patience and tend to scatter their energies. Their ingenuity and resourcefulness combine well with mechanical or engineering skills although they may change jobs frequently or have more than one occupation at a time. Naturally critical, these people have a ready wit, particularly sarcasm, and can be argumentative.

♂ in ♋ *Mars in Cancer*
Domestic life is always important to these individuals whether they seek

a home of their own at an early age or simply want their homes to be comfortable. Domestically, they are practical and constructive, but emotionally they are very intense and moody, sometimes relying far too heavily on their intuition.

♂ in ♌ Mars in Leo
These people are natural leaders and usually have very firm opinions of what is right and wrong; strongly passionate, they are possessive and jealous, yet they are socially popular, and have a natural flair for the dramatic arts. A sense of purpose underlies all their activities.

♂ in ♍ Mars in Virgo
This marks the skilled craftsman who organises his working environment well and gives his attention to detail. Precise and persevering, this individual can be ambitious and seek responsibility, yet not always maintain such a position because of being too pernickety. Friction with colleagues can arise due to misplaced ideals and a tendency to worry too much.

♂ in ♎ Mars in Libra
Team-work, associations with colleagues, and partnerships mean a lot to these subjects. Marriage may be sought more for companionship than for emotional and physical satisfaction although the libido is likely to be strong. As they are inclined to be temperamental their energies tend to fluctuate according to their mood.

♂ in ♏ Mars in Scorpio
Powerful, deep emotions tend to dominate this individual whose apparently ruthless manner indicates a strong survival instinct. Possessive and jealous in sexual and romantic relationships, such a person has a tendency to go to extremes in the pursuance of his or her ideals. They fight long and hard for their goals yet are rather secretive in their approach.

♂ in ♐ Mars in Sagittarius
Self-righteous, traditional, and a crusading spirit are the key qualities. In later years, religion, law or higher education may replace the somewhat misdirected zeal of youth when sport, travel and adventure tend to appeal. Enthusiasm underlies all the activities of these individuals who possess strong moral courage and convictions, despite their tendency to exaggerate.

♂ in ♑ Mars in Capricorn
This indicates materialism, ambition and practicality. Rational and decisive, these folk display a degree of independence in all their activities. Power suits them and is usually well employed whether they enter

the professions, politics or business. Fame is sometimes the objective of such individuals although financial considerations usually override everything else.

♂ in ♒ Mars in Aquarius
Freedom and independence are essential to these non-conformists. They have very quick reactions, superior intelligence and are somewhat unorthodox in their approach to most things. Unconventional, they do not take kindly to authority unless they respect those who wield it.

♂ in ♓ Mars in Pisces
Highly emotional, these subjects have a tendency to brood. Although sensitive and touchy, they often work quietly behind the scenes for the benefit of the less fortunate. Artistic expression is strong despite an overall laziness arising from a lack of self-confidence or direction which, unfortunately, may prevent them from attaining their aims in life.

(6) Jupiter

♃ in ♈ Jupiter in Aries
Self-sufficient, broad-minded and optimistic, these subjects possess an aura of honesty and integrity that inspires others to trust them. Impulsive at times, over-generous at others, they need to exercise more prudence. Sometimes the possibility of holding two careers at once will arise.

♃ in ♉ Jupiter in Taurus
This indicates a love of the good things of life, sometimes to the ment of health. Wealth may be acquired through sheer industry f⸺ folk need to feel materially secure. Patient and steady, asp¹ confident, they are inclined to be a little careless or to⸺ especially where monetary matters are concerned.

♃ in ♊ Jupiter in Gemini
These subjects are versatile and broadminded, with a that will lead them anywhere in the pursuit of kr⸺ restless, they dabble in most things, rarely speciali⸺ extraordinarily varied store of information. Al¹ tion appeal to these mentally alert individuals

♃ in ♋ Jupiter in Cancer
A good sense of business, good emotion⸺ position and receptive personality are ir⸺ and less fraught than the early year⸺

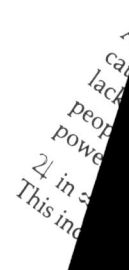

people follow careers in catering or allied subjects where their innate domesticity can be fulfilled.

♃ in ♌ Jupiter in Leo
Creativeness, expansiveness and self-confidence are the key qualities of these folk who often take up drama, sports or artistic pursuits professionally. They love luxury and pleasure and are attracted to all forms of pomp, ceremony and pageantry. Rather theatrical by temperament, they need to control their vanity.

♃ in ♍ Jupiter in Virgo
With their almost fanatical adherence to detail, these subjects are well-suited to scientific careers. Honest and idealistic, their excessive fastidiousness in matters of health, diet and appearance can detract from their basically genial, open personalities. Although occasionally lazy, they are dependable and work well as part of a team.

♃ in ♎ Jupiter in Libra
Easy-going and frank, these people have a strong sense of morality and fairness. However, a tendency to indulgence, laziness, and conceit can cause problems in close relationships. They can either be too reliant on others or totally independent. Convincing conversationalists, they can sell anything to anyone if they really try.

♃ in ♏ Jupiter in Scorpio
Intensely emotional, these subjects may be somewhat conceited and tend to overrate their abilities and capacity. They concentrate their best efforts on the material side of life and have a distinct flair for handling money, especially other people's. Shrewd, determined and sometimes aggressive, they are successful businessmen.

♃ in ♐ Jupiter in Sagittarius
Strongly philosophical, intellectual pursuits attract these individuals – religion, foreign affairs, traditions, the law, languages and the art of communication tend to fascinate them. Sometimes a love of animals and sporting activities are further attractions to these subjects who are inclined to gamble or take risks.

♃ in ♑ Jupiter in Capricorn
strong sense of duty, integrity, honesty and responsibility are indied. Any extravagance or waste of resources is disliked. An apparent of emotional warmth can be misleading although many of these le do tend to subjugate their personal desires in the pursuit of r, material possessions and social status.

♃ Jupiter in Aquarius
icates a self-willed, humane personality who can be tolerant up

to a point – behaviour can be erratic or indecisive depending on mood. Broadminded, such individuals can be relied upon to give an impartial opinion yet they are inclined to dissipate their energy and can, therefore, become too casual in outlook.

♃ in ♓ *Jupiter in Pisces*
A compassionate, humane and sympathetic nature is indicated. Many of these subjects feel a need to identify with a particular way of life or belief, something definite, and may retreat from everyday society in order to follow their goals. Others lack a mature outlook and tend to become unreliable, aimless and extravagant.

(7) Saturn

♄ in ♈ *Saturn in Aries*
Resourceful and self-willed, these people will succeed through their own efforts. Primarily concerned with their own aims, they may tend to lack consideration for the rights and wishes of those around them. Their persistence and conscious desire for security enable them to excel in most business ventures, particularly in the field of engineering or mechanics.

♄ in ♉ *Saturn in Taurus*
Methodical, reliable, steady and well-controlled, these subjects are efficient at their jobs, although they tend to be reserved and suspicious in their emotional relationships. Basically, they need to develop a more balanced outlook on life and to remember that obstinacy and stubbornness go hand in hand.

♄ in ♊ *Saturn in Gemini*
Profound, impartial, intellectual and rather lacking in emotional warmth, these people like well-ordered, disciplined lives, and shine best in careers that allow them to utilise their mental abilities. They can make excellent teachers although their tendency to be logical and austere at all times suggests that they may lack a sense of fun.

♄ in ♋ *Saturn in Cancer*
These individuals are emotionally sensitive and appear rather reserved. Usually, they have a very strong desire for security – both material and emotional – and may allow this trait to rule their lives. Although they often experience domestic problems, they can be surprisingly shrewd and successful in business.

♄ in ♌ *Saturn in Leo*
Reliable and loyal, these folk are very self-assured and can be rather dogmatic and imperious. If in positions of authority they are inclined to

be strict, although their innate sense of justice means that they are usually fair. However, selfishness or self-imposed restrictions can lead to emotional disappointments.

♄ in ♍ Saturn in Virgo
Severe, correct, prudent and practical, these subjects can become obsessive about detail. Very discreet, almost always conscientious, they have a strongly developed sense of responsibility about everything that they do. Emotionally serious, they tend to lack warmth and humour in their close relationships.

♄ in ♎ Saturn in Libra
This indicates a strong sense of fair play, tact and diplomacy. These individuals are very conscious of correct social behaviour and attitudes. They make good organisers and partners, both in business and marriage, and may become counsellors, mediators or negotiators.

♄ in ♏ Saturn in Scorpio
Executive ability and a sound business sense combine to make these people hard taskmasters. They have a tendency to judge others by their own high standards and may, therefore, expect too much – both from themselves and other people – with the result that they may become emotionally repressed.

♄ in ♐ Saturn in Sagittarius
Very conscious of personal status, these subjects tend to live at an intense intellectual pitch and sometimes lack sufficient understanding of the everyday problems of others. Often attracted to foreign countries and cultures, these folk are academically ambitious and frequently become known authorities in their chosen careers or professions.

♄ in ♑ Saturn in Capricorn
Worldly success, status, power and influence are strongly desired by these ambitious individuals who, more often than not, have all the traits necessary to achieve their aims. However, their patience can become dogged persistence and their determination can lead to a lack of impartiality, impairing their judgement.

♄ in ♒ Saturn in Aquarius
Reasonably practical in most ways, these folk concentrate their efforts on improving their minds and will take up any intellectual pursuits that give full reign to their imaginations. Although socially aspiring and humanitarian, they may be slightly selfish and emotionally intense.

♄ in ♓ Saturn in Pisces
Imagination, intuition, artistic creativity, compassion and sympathy combine to make these people rather complex personalities. Often they

are naturally shy which prevents them from expressing themselves properly. They can be introspective, with a tendency to relive past errors, and need quiet and solitude.

(8) Uranus

♅ in ♈ Uranus in Aries
Freedom of thought, word and deed is of paramount importance to these subjects. When on the defensive they can be blunt and very outspoken yet their extremely quick minds can defeat most opposition, even if only temporarily. Daring and resourceful, these people are not afraid to try anything new.

♅ in ♉ Uranus in Taurus
Determined, stubborn and quite clever in a practical way, these individuals often find new and different ways of organising people and things. Although financially astute as a rule, they do tend to gamble in an all or nothing style. Often artistic, they may utilise such talent in unusual ways.

♅ in ♊ Uranus in Gemini
Inventive and original, these folk are mentally active all the time although they do not always complete projects because they become bored quickly. They tend to rely too much on nervous energy and may suffer from tension as a result. They have a flair for all forms of communication and, very often, mechanical skills too.

♅ in ♋ Uranus in Cancer
Many with this placement leave home early in order to pursue their dreams, though they prefer to do so on amicable terms with their parents. They tend to fill their homes with all kinds of gadgetry and often hold distinctly untraditional views on domestic and family life. Intuitive and perceptive, they may be attracted to practical occultism.

♅ in ♌ Uranus in Leo
Emotionally rather unreliable, it is hard to pin these individuals down to their obligations and responsibilities although they do have genuine concern for the welfare of their friends. Strong-willed, bold and enterprising, they have good leadership qualities but can be stubborn and inflexible at times.

♅ in ♍ Uranus in Virgo
Unusual ideas concerning health and dietary matters are indicated. Always looking for new ways to get things done, these subjects may find it difficult to settle into routines of any kind. However, they do have

business talent, especially in those industries that develop and research new ideas. Emotionally erratic and changeable, they are very critical of themselves and others.

♅ in ♎ Uranus in Libra
These individuals have a tendency to make and break friendships very quickly. They may have unconventional attitudes towards marriage and emotional partnerships and may resent any form of restriction in these areas. Often, they hold unorthodox views regarding law and justice too. Any artistic talents are likely to be original.

♅ in ♏ Uranus in Scorpio
This is the mark of the all or nothing personality with powerful emotions just below the surface. Such a person is, of course, liable to display violent fits of temper. Adventurous, this individual makes an excellent friend but a formidable enemy.

♅ in ♐ Uranus in Sagittarius
Restless, adventurous and reckless at times, these folk are happy only when pursuing something new, and have a tendency to want to change what they consider to be outdated. Foreign travel, people and cultures are likely to appeal greatly to these subjects; scientific occultism may also attract.

♅ in ♑ Uranus in Capricorn
Good organisers, these individuals are usually considerate towards their close friends and colleagues but can be quite ruthless to opponents or rivals. Although they respect the traditional social order, they tend to be somewhat progressive as far as business and politics are concerned.

♅ in ♒ Uranus in Aquarius
This indicates a nature that requires change for the sake of the stimulation it may bring, or change based on a rebellious ideology. Humane, progressive, yet with a conscious tendency to exaggerate, these subjects value personal freedom above all else. Good organisers, they have the ability to put ideas to practical use but can be very stubborn.

♅ in ♓ Uranus in Pisces
These subjects are visionary, not very practical, and somewhat unreliable. They find the world a hard place to live in, due to their inability to face reality. Inclined to be secretive and imaginative, religion, mysticism and philosophical occultism usually attract them. They often possess highly original artistic talents – colour and music appeal greatly.

(9) Neptune

ψ in ♈ Neptune in Aries
This indicates a delicate and highly sensitive nature which may display occasional flashes of individualism. Mentally, this person is an adventurer and, spiritually, an awakener of old ideals, but incorporating new advances. Sometimes there are selfish motives behind the actions of these individuals. The danger lies in egotism and self-deception; more detachment and objectivity should be exercised.

ψ in ♉ Neptune in Taurus
Largely impractical in many ways, these folk are often sticklers for the old ways, beliefs and traditions. Not overly concerned with money they will, however, instinctively utilise whatever resources are available to improve their material well-being and that of others. Intuitive and sensitive, they need the constant reassurance of their loved ones.

ψ in ♊ in Gemini
Inspired, impressionable and quite complex, these subjects can be either broadminded and tolerant or narrow-minded and bigoted. Such complexities of nature mean, of course, that others find these individuals difficult to understand. Though sometimes rather muddle-headed and lacking in coherent thought, such people are capable of flashes of inspiration.

ψ in ♋ Neptune in Cancer
Emotionally sensitive, these individuals are very conscious of their domestic environment and the moods of those around them. Equally sensitive to the atmosphere of a particular place, nationalism may feature strongly in their lives. Rather introspective, religion and philosophy attract them and they may have pronounced mediumistic abilities.

ψ in ♌ Neptune in Leo
This indicates pronounced artistic talents and an attraction for the performing arts. Inclined to individualism and self-dramatisation, these subjects can be either soft-hearted and romantic or totally selfish and egotistical. They tend to impose upon others in order to promote their personal ambitions and can be idealistic rather than realistic.

ψ in ♍ Neptune in Virgo
Concern for the welfare of others and a desire to be useful in the community rules these folk, although this may be a misdirected or misunderstood aim. They can be very analytical and hypercritical of 'the system' and may experience difficulty in working as part of a team as they prefer to receive acknowledgement for their solo efforts.

Ψ in ♎ Neptune in Libra
A peace-loving and receptive nature is indicated. Broadly idealistic, there may be a tendency to be weak-willed and vacillating if the pursuit of pleasure takes on too great an importance. These subjects can be quite unrealistic in matters of love, sex and romance and are inclined to be idealistic, unworldly and lacking in positive drive.

Ψ in ♏ Neptune in Scorpio
Emotional intensity is the overriding factor here. As a result, personal morality may be extreme: these folk can either be quite hard, cruel and ruthless in order to achieve an aim, or they may be soft, gently persuasive and subtle. Naturally secretive, they are fascinated by the mysterious and often follow occult and metaphysical studies.

Ψ in ♐ Neptune in Sagittarius
A love of adventure and extravagance are shown by these expansive personalities who like to be on the move, to experience new things, to experiment. Philosophy and religion, education and politics may attract, but always from a radical or idealistic viewpoint. Intuitive and instinctive, these folk prefer simple things.

Ψ in ♑ Neptune in Capricorn
These subjects have good business sense and know intuitively what needs doing and when. Those who take up public careers may adopt double standards: the public figure becomes the exact opposite of the real, private individual. They should exercise caution when choosing partners because they tend to be too easily deceived by others.

Ψ in ♒ Neptune in Aquarius
This is the mark of the original personality but, in extreme cases, it can lead to eccentricity. Such individuals may be tempted to employ somewhat dubious methods in order to achieve their aims and should avoid the danger of allowing themselves to influence others by their actions. Despite this, such folk do have attractive personalities.

Ψ in ♓ Neptune in Pisces
Natural psychic abilities, coupled with artistic talents, are indicated here. The exclusive pursuit of physical pleasures may cause such subjects to adopt unconventional standards of behaviour. They are attracted to the mysterious and the unknown, revel in secrecy and have a tendency to be unrealistic about the more mundane aspects of life.

(10) Pluto

♇ in ♈ *Pluto in Aries*
This indicates an extremely assertive personality. Such people have the capacity for sheer hard work, a pioneering spirit and are quite prepared to tear down the old in order to make way for the new. They have leadership qualities, but can be over-ambitious and should avoid allowing their desire to succeed to override all other considerations.

♇ in ♉ *Pluto in Taurus*
Materially acquisitive, these folk are likely to experience sudden and extreme reversals of financial fortune. They have a good grasp of business and a strong desire to be in control at all times. They resent the interference of others and can be quite vindictive in their efforts to exact revenge. Sensual, they may be over possessive of their partners.

♇ in ♊ *Pluto in Gemini*
These subjects have tremendous mental vitality, originality and perception. Well-established techniques and long-held beliefs may be challenged in order to institute a new order because their enquiring minds are always seeking fresh ground to conquer. Mentally restless, they like to communicate their knowledge to others and many of them follow more than one career.

♇ in ♋ *Pluto in Cancer*
Emotional expression is very strongly marked in these subjects who are very conscious of family and domestic commitments. Traditionalists at heart, many of them enter politics in order to satisfy their nationalistic feelings. They have strong opinions, to which they will adhere doggedly, and often join groups or associations that are in sympathy with their views.

♇ in ♌ *Pluto in Leo*
A love of power and the desire to rule are indicated. These people demand – and usually receive – the loyalty of their friends as a right. Egotistical, they can be arrogant as they are exceptionally determined and have the will to win at all times. Their weakest point is their sexual appetite which, if uncontrolled, can overpower them.

♇ in ♍ *Pluto in Virgo*
Inquisitive, assertive and zealous, these subjects enjoy acquiring specialised knowledge which they can put to practical use. Although many of them concentrate their efforts on improving society, they can be overly critical of themselves and others, thus causing friction. They may become obsessed with diet, health and hygiene and shun orthodox medicine and 'artificial' foods.

♇ in ♎ *Pluto in Libra*
Law, justice and social issues interest these folk who often take up careers in psychology or counselling. The welfare of others is of primary concern to such individuals and they will go out of their way to implement changes which they believe will be beneficial. They are naturally sympathetic and peace-loving and abhor violence.

♇ in ♏ *Pluto in Scorpio*
These subjects will display exceptional tenacity and endurance when pursuing an ambition. They have leadership qualities but may abuse them, sometimes using other people for personal gain. Despite this they are capable of undertaking the toughest tasks for the benefit of others. Emotionally intense, their sex drive is likely to be strong.

♇ in ♐ *Pluto in Sagittarius*
A desire to implement changes in traditional beliefs and ideals may lead these individuals into the realms of abstract philosophy. Ever anxious to learn and to increase their knowledge, they tend to pursue their educational interests to the detriment of their relationships and can become rather isolated as a consequence.

♇ in ♑ *Pluto in Capricorn*
These people are usually dedicated to their careers or professions and have an overriding ambition to succeed, possibly at any cost, and may 'bend the rules' in order to achieve their aims. Impatient and inconsiderate at times, they may have a tendency to be rather dictatorial.

♇ in ♒ *Pluto in Aquarius*
Intensely interested in scientific and technological matters, these reformists seldom lack original ideas – even if these are difficult to implement. Anything new or challenging will attract their fertile minds and imaginations. Although rather demanding in their personal relationships, these individuals set much store by friendship.

♇ in ♓ *Pluto in Pisces*
This indicates rather a solitary personality, profound and intellectual, but with great magnetic appeal. These individuals have investigative natures, love puzzles and problems, possessing the patience to solve them. They are frequently attracted to the occult, philosophy or any inspirational subject. Very creative and artistically talented, these people love to explore new mediums of expression.

CHAPTER 5
The Planets in the Twelve Houses

The significance of each planet in each house

(1) The Sun

☉ *in the 1st House*
This signifies strong self-assurance, will-power and good vitality. Potential leaders, these individuals have clear-cut ambitions, are power conscious and tend to ignore the opinions of others. When the Sun occupies the 1st House, it often means that the Sun sign is also the rising sign or Ascendant. This will tend to over-emphasise the sign and the house with the result that the subject's personality may suffer some imbalance.

☉ *In the 2nd House*
Emphasis will be placed on possessions and financial security. These subjects will use money sensibly and, unless very careless, should always be comfortably off. The sign on the cusp of this house may indicate the manner in which they are likely to make their living.

☉ *in the 3rd House*
Travel and communication of all kinds are likely to appeal greatly to these changeable, restless, and curious individuals. They may, however, need to learn self-discipline because their active minds tend to flit from subject to subject and they can lack patience. Any brothers and sisters will play an important role in their lives.

☉ *in the 4th House*
Domestic and family matters are likely to dominate the lives of these subjects who may also show an interest in local politics, ecology and natural resources. They are likely to appear somewhat reserved in their personal relationships due to their very impressionable natures but should find later life less difficult than the earlier years.

☉ *in the 5th House*
Slightly domineering and rather theatrical, these enthusiastic and cheer-

ful people have a wide range of interests and often get on very well with children. Although their active self-confidence may lead them to take unnecessary risks, they are temperamentally suited to careers in the arts, entertainment and sport.

○ *in the 6th House*
Although hard-working and with good organising ability, these individuals could encounter difficulties in their working relationships because of their punctilious attitude which can become too pronounced. However, they frequently do well in careers where their natural interest in health and diet can be utilised fully.

○ *in the 7th House*
This Solar house position is good for partnerships of all kinds. Public relations, dealing with superiors and personal relationships are emphasised. Marriage is likely to be important to such subjects although they may have a tendency to be too selective and not to be really happy with the chosen mate, despite the prosperity such alliances often bring.

○ *in the 8th House*
Will-power and financial ability are accentuated. These individuals are best suited to careers where they handle other people's money, such as insurance or accountancy. Naturally studious, they are often attracted to philosophical or metaphysical subjects. If possible, they should avoid litigation as this could prove troublesome and unfavourable.

○ *in the 9th House*
An interest in foreign affairs, further education, long-distance travel and the advancement of social status are well marked. Many of these subjects hold deep religious feelings and strong moral convictions. They are likely to be somewhat idealistic and may experience flashes of inspiration that prove materially profitable in the long run.

○ *in the 10th House*
This signifies strong vocational motivation, a serious disposition, and high moral principles. Such people will work hard to promote their careers, often achieving authority early in life as a result. Professionally ambitious, these subjects are likely to have the determination necessary to progress in their chosen careers.

○ *in the 11th House*
Social welfare and group activities are emphasised. Yet, despite their pronounced humanitarian leanings, these individuals sometimes use others in order to achieve their goals and are particularly successful at eliciting the help of influential people. They are very observant, utilising this trait to good effect when pursuing their aims.

☉ *in the 12th House*
A shy, reserved, introspective disposition is indicated. Lack of self-expression can lead to difficulties in personal relationships, particularly partnerships, which can present problems. However, such subjects often find fulfilment through service to others and many pursue careers in the caring professions.

(2) The Moon

☽ *in the 1st House*
Changeable and moody, often influenced by early childhood experiences, this person will feel a need to share life with others. Over eager to please, probably hasty or rash, such an individual is likely to venture 'where angels fear to tread', particularly in pursuit of personal ambitions.

☽ *in the 2nd House*
Although not mean, financial security is important to these people because their general well-being is dependent on material comforts. They have keen business sense, especially for any form of investment, although some of them may be inclined to cling to outmoded methods or systems.

☽ *in the 3rd House*
A tendency to daydream, a vivid imagination and an almost insatiable curiosity are indicated. Yet, despite their wide range of knowledge and undoubted mental agility, these subjects are inclined to worry unnecessarily over trivia. Also, their lives may be influenced unduly by their brothers and sisters.

☽ *in the 4th House*
Home life will be very important to these individuals who often have a strong attachment to children, and there may be many changes of residence. The past may fascinate or play an important role in their lives which tend to become more settled and relaxed after middle age.

☽ *in the 5th House*
Emotional instability and an over-active imagination are the mark of this Lunar position. However, it is good for sporting interests and the subject may have a 'lucky touch' in financial affairs. This person's partner may find that he or she takes on most of the responsibilities of the relationship.

☽ *in the 6th House*
Concern with health and dietary matters is emphasised, which may be

reflected in the subject's choice of career. Often, such a person will undertake work that is a form of service to others although the occupation may be changed quite frequently – according to mood.

☽ *in the 7th House*
This Lunar position is good for dealing with the public and almost any form of relationship except, perhaps, for partnerships. Business capability is well marked because, despite any outward show of 'softness', this individual is likely to be quite shrewd.

☽ *in the 8th House*
Ambitious, perhaps a little ruthless and lacking in tact, this subject's emotions may be governed by his strong physical passions. A fascination for finance may well be reflected in the chosen career although psychic phenomena are also likely to prove of interest to such a person.

☽ *in the 9th House*
This indicates an irregular life-style – travel, study, philosophy – and relationships may be subject to change and disruption. However, such people may well have one particular overriding interest which will dominate their lives – perhaps a hobby that could be utilised for earning a living.

☽ *in the 10th House*
With an overruling desire to succeed, these ambitious individuals may neglect their personal lives in the pursuit of their professional aims. Yet, despite their seriousness and wish for status, which may lead others to regard them as 'hard', these subjects have sympathetic natures beneath their outer shells.

☽ *in the 11th House*
This marks a clever, original mind – someone who will shine when in the company of others and who enjoys group activities. However, periods of isolation may be necessary in order for this person to 'recharge batteries' and he may have few friends but many acquaintances.

☽ *in the 12th House*
Moody and withdrawn, these subjects often feel that the world owes them a living. Shy, very emotional and impressionable, such personalities are inclined to drift through life. However, they usually show concern for others and this trait may be reflected in their careers.

(3) Mercury

☿ in the 1st House
Self-centred, but fairly logical in their general approach to life, these people nearly always have enquiring minds and above average intelligence. They are observant, have a ready wit and are rarely lost for words. Travel is likely to play an important role in their lives, whether for business or pleasure.

☿ in the 2nd House
Methodical, original and inventive, these subjects know how to protect their interests because of their innate financial ability and good business sense. Often, their management potential will manifest early in their careers which are likely to involve communication, perhaps in an advisory capacity, and financial dealings.

☿ in the 3rd House
Placed here, Mercury stimulates the mental processes to such a degree that overall intelligence will be well above average. Adaptable, active and lively, such subjects will tend to live on nervous energy, which could undermine their health. Travel will probably be an integral part of their jobs, such as in salesmanship, for example.

☿ in the 4th House
These people are inclined to accumulate possessions that will assist them to further their interests and many of them will work from home. They have natural curiosity – even if only to keep up with the news of the day – and their memories are usually good. One potential problem area lies in inter-family relationships which may be·poor.

☿ in the 5th House
Although analytical and critical, these folk are also dramatic, rather inclined to take risks and are attracted to almost any challenging pursuit, including speculative ventures. They have a knack for communicating with children and work well with youngsters.

☿ in the 6th House
Methodical and efficient, these subjects seldom lack financial security and often enter professions requiring specialised skills, such as science or medicine. Emotionally cool and a little prudish, they tend to be over critical and dislike anything that is not orderly, logical and practical.

☿ in the 7th House
This indicates a marked aptitude for communicating with others and these individuals are well-suited to salesmanship, negotiation and arbitration, public relations, etc. Although they do require periods of solitude, they need constant mental stimulation and function best when in the company of others.

☿ *in the 8th House*
Fascinated by secrecy, mystery and intrigue, these folk are adept at realising the motives of others and can usually forestall any adverse behaviour that is directed towards them. Naturally passionate, they are inclined to hold grudges and seek revenge if they feel they have been slighted.

☿ *in the 9th House*
With this placing, the accent is on the acquisition of knowledge, often in specialist subjects. It is the mark of the eternal student, those who wish to understand fully everything about their chosen field. There is a danger, however, that these people may become dogmatic and intellectually arrogant.

☿ *in the 10th House*
This indicates a marked facility for dealing with those in authority. These individuals are very concerned with everything that is intellectually stimulating, are able to communicate ideas to others and often realise their ambitions early in life because of their willingness to assume responsibility.

☿ *in the 11th House*
Original, objective, great lovers of truth and reason, these people make good students as well as teachers. Philosophical and humanitarian, they are interested in learning what makes others tick and often become involved in group activities, especially those concerned with social issues.

☿ *in the 12th House*
Creative and imaginative, these folk are full of ideas but may lack the ability to put them into practice. Kind, charitable and humorous, they may be attracted to the arts or entertainment because, although shy, they are not adverse to appearing or performing in public.

(4) Venus

♀ *in the 1st House*
This is indicative of artistic talent. These personable individuals have a friendly, cheerful manner, are often physically attractive and fashion-conscious. They may, however, be somewhat self-indulgent, rather lazy, and overly concerned with their social lives, to the detriment of their other interests.

♀ *in the 2nd House*
Social status means much to these subjects, as does the acquisition of possessions, but they may tend to be extravagant. Basically, however

they are financially shrewd and should benefit from business transactions, speculation and investment. Emotionally, they are constant and faithful.

♀ *in the 3rd House*
Travel, communications and social affairs are emphasised. Many of these folk follow careers connected with the written or spoken word. They tend to look for mental affinity with their partners, rather than physical attraction, and will remain loyal – for a time. Almost always likeable, they can, however, be changeable.

♀ *in the 4th House*
These subjects must have congenial, comfortable and, wherever possible, luxurious surroundings because their domestic environment is very important to them. They have close family ties, and may be concerned with local issues and politics but are inclined to be a little choosey in their social relationships.

♀ *in the 5th House*
Popular and likeable, these people enjoy the social round and have a wide circle of friends and acquaintances yet may experience many affairs before they settle down as they tend to confuse sex with love. Friendly and outgoing, they are attracted to the theatre, music and the arts generally.

♀ *in the 6th House*
A preoccupation with hygiene and health may lead these individuals to worry unnecessarily. Although they mostly have very high moral standards, promiscuity is not unknown with Venus in this house. These folk need harmonious working conditions and many of them are artistically inclined and may pursue these interests in a career or as a hobby.

♀ *in the 7th House*
This indicates a warm, sympathetic personality: the type of person who knows how to enjoy life gracefully and to the full. An understanding nature and concern for fairness could lead to an interest or career in psychology or counselling. Loyal and faithful in personal relationships, an early marriage is probable.

♀ *in the 8th House*
Romantically imaginative and intensely sensuous, these folk may pursue such pleasures to the neglect of all else; however, jealousy and possessiveness can cause problems and loss. Often, they gain financially through their partners, thus acquiring improved social status.

♀ in the 9th House
Highly idealistic and studious, these people may take up residence abroad in order to further their education and many choose a marriage partner of another race, creed or culture. Generally, they take life steadily and seriously so are well able to cope with any minor difficulties that such mixed marriages can bring.

♀ in the 10th House
This planetary position points to material wealth although this may not necessarily result in personal happiness. Socially ambitious, these subjects work and play hard to achieve their aims. Due to their respect and admiration for influential people, they get on well with those in positions of power and authority.

♀ in the 11th House
This indicates an outgoing, progressive personality whose warm, friendly manner attracts a wide circle of friends and acquaintances. A respect for personal freedom combined with diplomacy and tact makes such an individual a first-class negotiator or mediator and any type of advisory or counselling work would be likely to appeal.

♀ in the 12th House
Kindly and sympathetic, these folk make loyal friends although their innate shyness can sometimes prevent them from achieving the affection of those they admire most. This inability to satisfy their emotional needs can lead to feelings of inadequacy and frustration. Occultism may well attract these gentle, modest people.

(5) Mars

♂ in the 1st House
Competitive, self-confident and ambitious, these individuals have the capacity to work hard in order to achieve their aims. Extroverts, their manner can be a bit aggressive due to the directness of their speech and actions. Too impatient and impulsive to always heed necessary safety precautions, they are potentially accident-prone.

♂ in the 2nd House
Competitive, tenacious, practical and financially competent, this subject has the necessary qualifications to set up in business for himself. He or she is able to sell ideas successfully but is obstinate and persistent and should avoid the pitfall of aggressive salesmanship. Materialistic, possessive and sensuous, this person can be inclined to outbursts of bad temper when aroused.

♂ in the 3rd House
This indicates an assertive but somewhat contradictory character. Highly mobile, such an individual may, however, be a reckless or careless driver due to thoughtlessness and a natural inclination to take risks. Although attracted to occupations involving communication, this person's direct, even caustic speech can mar personal relationships.

♂ in the 4th House
Very moody, these subjects need to find an outlet for their creative and constructive talents. As they are deeply concerned with their immediate environment, home decorating, gardening or local politics often provides fulfilment. Domestic instability is the danger here, probably arising from disputes in the immediate family or long-standing disagreements with parents or in-laws.

♂ in the 5th House
High-spirited and enterprising, these individuals have good leadership qualities. They get on well with children, make good teachers, particularly of the very young, and many have an interest in competitive sports. As they are very emotional and sensual, they may allow their strong passions to lead them into numerous love affairs, whether they are married or single.

♂ in the 6th House
Conscientious and hard-working, though not always robust, these subjects excel in occupations that require precision and an eye for detail; many of them enter research, medicine, catering or the service industries. Often attracted to industrial politics, this interest sometimes leads to unrest and difficulties in their working environment.

♂ in the 7th House
This planetary position is excellent for dealing with the public and for partnerships of all kinds. A lively, sociable attitude usually leads to a wide-ranging circle of friends and acquaintances. Naturally competitive, these folk are very high-spirited and may have difficulty controlling their enthusiasms. On the positive side, they are tactful and diplomatic, while on the other hand they can be contentious and aggressive.

♂ in the 8th House
Powerful, deep-seated but easily aroused emotions are indicated here. These subjects tend to be secretive about their actions, will not tolerate opposition and will react to any form of interference. They are financially competent, dealing expertly with other people's money or with joint finances. An interest in occult or psychic phenomena is probable.

♂ *in the 9th House*
Activity is the keynote – travel, exploration, sports and military service are likely to attract these people who are concerned equally with the acquisition of material possessions and the knowledge of those subjects that interest them. They may, indeed, be a little fanatical about some things yet, despite any narrowness of vision, are loyal and trustworthy.

♂ *in the 10th House*
Ambitious and hard-working, these individuals are good organisers, practical and willing to take on responsibility yet able to delegate sensibly. Realistic, independent and competent, they are competitive, can be ruthless when necessary and will fight all comers in their efforts to achieve status, authority and influence.

♂ *in the 11th House*
This indicates a strongly independent personality – someone who is determined to retain his or her individuality whatever the circumstances or the cost. Group activities are likely to stimulate and attract this person's interest but close personal relationships are less likely to survive his or her abhorrence of long-term commitments and slightly superficial characteristics.

♂ *in the 12th House*
Mars in this position can create certain inconsistences of behaviour and attitude. These subjects are nearly always secretive, tend to lack self-control and are inclined to change their minds and beliefs for no apparent reason. Unreliable and moody, many crave the stimulation offered by heavy drinking, smoking, drugs or sex.

(6) Jupiter

♃ *in the 1st House*
Frank, honest and trustworthy, these people inspire confidence and respect. Usually responsible and well-balanced personalities, many achieve success early in life. They should, however, avoid complacency because self-indulgence could affect health detrimentally. Basically upright characters, they may hold strong moral or religious convictions.

♃ *in the 2nd House*
Good business ability is indicated by this planetary position. Although inattention to detail and lack of foresight may lead to some financial loss, these subjects should achieve their ambitions, wealth, material possessions and prestige, once they have overcome their youthful tendency to spend money almost as fast as it comes in.

♃ *in the 3rd House*
Emphasis falls on communications of all kinds – the written and spoken word, travel, transportation, etc. A facile, carefree manner may be misinterpreted as superficiality because this individual craves constant stimulation. Alert and active, he or she needs to occupy mind and body with new interests, new people and new activities or will become bored.

♃ *in the 4th House*
This subject's home and family will be the focal point of his or her life. Such a person will spend as much time as possible in the domestic environment, perhaps even using it for business purposes, and close relationships will therefore take on added significance. This reliance on a settled home environment could result in ill-health should the status quo be upset.

♃ *in the 5th House*
The creative arts, sports and anything involving children will produce the best results from these self-confident, sociable people. Usually, they make successful marriages – stable and happy – but should let their partners handle their joint monetary affairs to avoid unnecessary hardship because they tend to be poor financial managers.

♃ *in the 6th House*
This is the mark of service and the welfare of others will be of prime importance to people who have Jupiter in this house position. Hardworking, with a capacity for detail, these conscientious folk make excellent employees or employers; many of them enter the medical professions, welfare or social services or catering.

♃ *in the 7th House*
Easy-going, optimistic and with a strong sense of justice, these individuals are noted for their honesty and fair dealing in business matters although they can be susceptible to pie-in-the-sky schemes. This planetary position indicates a good marriage but the subject will have to work hard to keep it that way because of a tendency to take things and people for granted.

♃ *in the 8th House*
An interest in occult matters linked with strong religious beliefs is likely. Materialistic, and ruthless in business, especially in financial affairs, such people may misuse power in order to achieve domination over others. They need to develop self-discipline and a sense of responsibility because they tend to be extravagant and self-indulgent, particularly in the pursuit of sexual pleasures.

♃ *in the 9th House*
Foreign travel, cultures and customs are likely to appeal to these serious-

minded, studious people. Avid in their search for further knowledge, they often become teachers or lecturers themselves. They are deeply concerned with philosophical, religious and moral issues but can become somewhat narrow-minded or bigoted.

♃ *in the 10th House*
Egocentric, these individuals will actively seek power and influence in order to promote their self-image. Ambitious and able, they are more than likely to achieve their goals and, somewhat surprisingly perhaps, rarely fail to live up to expectations. However, should a fall from grace occur, these people will regard the event as catastrophic.

♃ *in the 11th House*
Although socially successful and popular, these subjects may not always be completely honest and tend to use others for their own ends; they seek the friendship and support of influential people, often with ulterior motives in mind. They are more attracted to the sciences than the arts and many of them enter the scientific professions.

♃ *in the 12th House*
Idealistic, impractical and unrealistic, these folk tend to live in a dream world. Introspective, perhaps lonely, they dislike direct responsibility and work best in the background, often for the benefit of others, in such places as hospitals, institutions or charitable organisations.

---

(7) Saturn

♄ *in the 1st House*
Rather serious-minded and hard-working, these individuals seem to acquire responsibility whether they like it or not. Austere, they may appear to lack emotional warmth because they build a wall around themselves and few, if any, will be allowed to penetrate this barrier. They are also very self-willed.

♄ *in the 2nd House*
These people seem to work hard for very little material success although they sometimes achieve financial security in later life. Shrewd in business matters, they make formidable opponents because they leave very little to chance. Emotionally shy, they tend not to trust other people.

♄ *in the 3rd House*
Overly cautious, not very adaptable or flexible, these subjects prefer to be left to their own devices in both business and personal matters. Practical and realistic, schemes and plans will be judged by their

usefulness. Any brothers and sisters are likely to feature prominently in their lives.

♄ in the 4th House
These people are extremely sensitive, which could cause problems in their emotional relationships, particularly close family ties. Often, they are saddled with responsibilities early in life, especially domestic duties, and they frequently follow occupations concerned with the home, gardening, farming or the building trades.

♄ in the 5th House
Executive ability and good business sense can lead these subjects to enter politics or finance. Even when young, their friends tend to be useful social contacts who will help promote their business interests. Emotionally inhibited, they tend to avoid close personal attachments.

♄ in the 6th House
This position implies specialised occupational skills. Thorough and cautious, these individuals leave little to chance and take a serious approach to life in general; indeed, their responsible attitude often makes them appear older than they are. Naturally quiet and reserved, these people are thoughtful and reliable.

♄ in the 7th House
Relationships and partnerships of all kinds are emphasised although these folk may not marry until quite late in life. They are good planners because of their ability to allow for the unexpected but can be a little too serious-minded for their own good and may be unable to relax properly except when working on a favourite project.

♄ in the 8th House
These careful, serious and responsible individuals are good at handling financial affairs and official matters, such as tax and insurance. Esoteric subjects interest them and they may take up philosophical or religious studies. At the very least, they are likely to be attracted by occultism and psychic phenomena.

♄ in the 9th House
This position indicates someone who will attain power and authority in later life through sheer hard work. Rather reserved and lonely, business and travel will provide most of life's pleasures, particulary if these result in trips abroad. Religion and education are likely to play an important role in this fair-minded person's life.

♄ in the 10th House
Concentration, moral integrity and strong will-power help these people to reach the top of the tree early in their careers. However, they need to

exercise caution in order to maintain their exalted positions as any inattention may allow others to oust them from power because they are rather susceptible emotionally.

♄ *in the 11th House*
These individuals may cultivate the friendship of those older than themselves because, subconsciously, they seek out those who can further their ambitions. They are sociable and charming, although they are inclined to use people, and flourish in group activities, making loyal dependable friends.

♄ *in the 12th House*
Timid, moody and sensitive, these people are usually their own worst enemies. They crave the affection of others but their retiring natures prevent them from making friends easily and they may avoid social contact. They tend to stay in the background, often entering professions where they can help the less fortunate.

(8) Uranus

♅ *in the 1st House*
Unusual and eccentric at times, this individual's mind is never still. Versatile, restless, always on the look-out for something new or untried, such a person can show surprising streaks of stubbornness and ruthlessness just as easily as humanity and flexibility. Intelligent and intuitive, behavioural patterns can be quite changeable and unpredictable.

♅ *in the 2nd House*
This signifies financial ups and downs, largely due to risking cash in speculative and doubtful ventures. These subjects are not always conventional in their approach to monetary matters. They tend to borrow or lend indiscriminately and may commit unavailable funds to a scheme that appeals to them.

♅ *in the 3rd House*
Restless, impractical and changeable, these people prefer to learn by experience – despite the obvious risks. Original, inventive and intuitive, they have a humane streak which can manifest at any time, although they can appear quite impersonal and impractical on occasion. Sometimes, these folk will change their fundamental life-styles on reaching middle-age.

♅ *in the 4th House*
This person's changeable nature and desire to travel could result in a

somewhat unsettled domestic life, especially in youth. Some friction with parents and many changes of residence are indicated although this inventive, original individual has the ability to make a home almost anywhere and will settle down more in later life.

♅ *in the 5th House*
These artistic and creative individuals are unconventional, preferring the company of those with unusual personalities. Adventurous and impulsive, they are rather extravagant and tend to be attracted to risky ventures. Serious problems could arise unless they learn to control their sexual urges and their inclination to demand too much freedom of expression.

♅ *in the 6th House*
Probably interested in fringe medicine, electronics and engineering – areas offering opportunities to develop new techniques – this person may find it difficult to settle down to a routine occupation. Analytical and mentally alert, such a subject would do best in an intellectually stimulating job, marketing for instance.

♅ *in the 7th House*
This indicates curious ideas regarding marriage and emotional relationships. Extremely independent and wilful, yet intellectual and humanitarian, these subjects may choose a career or life-style that places them in the public eye. Success will depend on how much these people manage to learn through personal experience.

♅ *in the 8th House*
An eventful life is indicated. These folk are interested in the odd and the mysterious, whether in daily life or relationships, and may be as attracted to esoteric studies as they are to unusual sexual encounters. This fascination for the curious and an impulsive nature can result in financially, physically and emotionally dangerous situations.

♅ *in the 9th House*
Philosophical and idealistic, this individual will be interested in educational, religious and political reform. Adventurous and impulsive, such a person will be attracted by anything new and unusual. Inclined to jump to conclusions at times, he or she is undisciplined, easily distracted and needs to cultivate method and control.

♅ *in the 10th House*
Original and gifted, strong-willed and determined, these subjects have the energy necessary to pursue their careers in an almost fanatical manner although some of them may be inclined to dissipate their energies. A little unconventional, they may not always agree with authority and yet have first-class leadership qualities which they will exercise if given the opportunity.

♅ *in the 11th House*
Intuitive, compassionate, progressive and sociable, these people shine most when in company. Group activities attract them although they tend to make and break friendships quickly, often for no apparent reason. Usually, they will try anything once for the sake of experience. When older, they often become interested in astrology and the occult.

♅ *in the 12th House*
Highly imaginative and perhaps a little eccentric, these individuals are basically impractical and not very trusting though they can be trusted implicitly with the secrets of others. Fascinated by the unknown, they are likely to be interested in occult research and practice and many of them will pursue such subjects.

---

(9) Neptune

♆ *in the 1st House*
These sensitve, intuitive people are born dreamers and somewhat impractical although many of them are artistically or musically talented. Gentle and easy-going, they attract a wide circle of friends, including the more unorthodox, and may lack the will-power to resist drugs, drink or sexual excesses.

♆ *in the 2nd House*
Idealistic and tactful, but not particularly robust, these subjects seek friendship and harmony in their surroundings. They appreciate the beauty of colour and design, often collecting or investing in objets d'art or antiques, but they should avoid direct financial speculation as they are not good at handling money.

♆ *in the 3rd House*
This indicates a highly imaginative, impressionable personality. Such an individual may well use his or her talents as an entertainer or enter a career that places him in the public eye. However, there may be a tendency to drift through life due to a lack of concentrated effort and an inclination to have too many interests.

♆ *in the 4th House*
These subjects are natural home-makers who need a 'retreat' where they can go to recharge their batteries and escape the rigours of pursuing unfulfilled ambitions. Childhood memories often mean a lot to these emotionally vulnerable folk who enjoy the countryside.

♆ *in the 5th House*
These highly emotional subjects are likely to be attracted to the performing arts and other creative activites. They have good planning

ability and can inspire others with their enthusiasm but lack the practicality to make their schemes work. Their affections, too, may be misdirected and this could lead to problems in relationships.

Ψ *in the 6th House*
The welfare of others is of prime importance to these sensitive, introspective folk who often devote their lives to some form of service to others. Although they tend to suffer from psychosomatic illnesses, many of them pursue careers in medicine or allied occupations and work in hospitals or similar institutions.

Ψ *in the 7th House*
Intuitive and imaginative, often artistically or musically talented, these individuals tend to go their own way according to the mood of the moment. Somewhat unorthodox, they are inclined to ignore conventions and may impose their ideas on others, particularly in their close relationships.

Ψ *in the 8th House*
Moody and idealistic, these people need to develop a more practical attitude towards everyday life in order to cope with the problems that can arise on a mundane level, particularly financial. Very imaginative and intuitive, they are often attracted to occultism, religious, philosophical or spiritual studies.

Ψ *in the 9th House*
Although tolerant, religious, impressionable and intuitive, these folk can be fanatical in some of their beliefs. Sometimes impractical and neglectful of education, they may lack discrimination due to an inability to face up to reality. Problems with in-laws may arise.

Ψ *in the 10th House*
This is a good house position for actors, artists and musicians because it tends to bring the subject before the public eye through an unusual gift or talent. However, ambitions should be curbed because underhandedness or unreliability could result in a disastrous fall from favour.

Ψ *in the 11th House*
Often too idealistic to be practical, these folk lack self-confidence and discernment. They seek the constant admiration and reassurance of others but tend to lack the ability to choose their friends sensibly. As they are easily influenced by the opinions and life-styles of others, they may drift into a Bohemian way of life.

Ψ *in the 12th House*
These philosophical, idealistic individuals are usually interested in religious, occult or spiritual matters. Often artistically or musically

gifted, they are attracted to the arts, drama and the written word. Rather reserved by nature, they are inclined to be inhibited and need to choose their partners carefully.

(10) Pluto

P in the 1st House
Extremely intense and determined, these people are very ambitious, and perhaps a little ruthless. Strong-willed, such individuals have the ability to control their lives and usually achieve their aims. They may have few close friends due to their serious, rather aloof manner.

P in the 2nd House
Resourceful and intuitive, with an excellent financial and business sense, this subject is likely to set great store by material possessions, perhaps to the point of greed and selfishness. Authoritative, this person has great depth of feeling and may tend to try to influence all those who come within his or her orbit.

P in the 3rd House
This indicates the born investigator – someone with good powers of observation, intellectual prowess, an analytical mind and the ability to communicate at all levels. However, a domineering attitude and strong opinions could mar close family relationships.

P in the 4th House
An aptitude for research – plus an interest in nature – could lead this individual to specialise in ecology, conservation or allied subjects. Family matters are of equal importance to such a person although there may be some difficulty in relating to one or both parents due to decided views on domestic issues.

P in the 5th House
Competitive pastimes, such as games or sports, are likely to appeal to these people's need to prove their worth to others. Serious and rather intense, such individuals can become obsessed by the physical side of life and need to learn self-restraint, particularly as their sexual appetite may be quite difficult to control.

P in the 6th House
Investigative and research projects tend to attract these self-reliant folk who prefer to complete tasks without interruption or interference from others. Long, concentrated hours of effort can result in mental and physical exhaustion, so there is a need for them to watch their health carefully.

♇ *in the 7th House*
Relationships of all kinds are emphasised by this planetary position and there is an overriding need to have a partner with whom to share life fully. Loyal and faithful, these strong-willed, level-headed people are often attracted to the law, psychology, public life or any occupation requiring responsibility.

♇ *in the 8th House*
Clairvoyance, metaphysical and occult subjects are likely to appeal to these folk who have a tendency to investigate thoroughly anything that takes their fancy. They should take care not to become too intense, however, for they are inclined to have an 'all or nothing' attitude towards most things and can be rather possessive.

♇ *in the 9th House*
This is the mark of crusading spirits – those who are uninterested in daily trivia but will pursue their overriding ambitions with determination and enthusiasm, sometimes to the point of exhaustion. These subjects have a profound interest in people and what makes them tick and are concerned with improving humanity's lot.

♇ *in the 10th House*
These ambitious folk have aspirations for authority, and often achieve positions of responsibility early in life due to their ability to manipulate others. They should, however, curb any inclination to become overbearing or dictatorial or they could mar their personal relationships, particularly close ties.

♇ *in the 11th House*
Sociable and with strong humanitarian ideals, these individuals usually attract a wide circle of acquaintances but have few close friends as they are inclined to be lone wolves. Often able to solicit the help and advice of influential people, they can become too determined to implement their plans and objectives.

♇ *in the 12th House*
This planetary position indicates a preoccupation with the unknown: the occult and the mysterious attract these secretive people, as do natural healing and alternative therapies. However, they tend to lack genuine concern for others and are likely to make and break agreements and friendships without compunction.

CHAPTER 6
Aspects and their significance

A brief outline of the significance of the major aspects in a natal chart

☉ ☌ ☽ (1) **The Conjunctions**

This aspect emphasises the Sun sign. Impulsive, active and creative, the subject may tend to concentrate his efforts in one particular area of life to the neglect of other issues. It can indicate a temperamental nature.

☉ ☌ ☿

This indicates good powers of observation and perception, a high degree of intellect and strong will-power. The individual may, however, have a rather subjective outlook and not be very flexible in his or her attitude.

☉ ☌ ♀

A cheeful, magnetic personality is indicated – someone who is optimistic and friendly, especially towards the young. Emotionally forceful and idealistic, such a person may be artistically or musically talented.

☉ ☌ ♂

Aggressive, energetic, assertive and not without courage, this subject is enthusiastic and emotionally intense. However, such a self-willed person may be rather prone to be intransigent and not always as tactful as is necessary.

☉ ☌ ♃

An expansive, magnaminous and enthusiastic nature is indicated. Executive ability will be backed up by natural pride, inherent talent, plus the will to succeed and thereby improve social standing.

☉ ☌ ♄

This signifies strong self-discipline and a rather serious, independent temperament. Very hard-working, such people may feel limited by their inability to express themselves fully and could become loners.

☉ ☌ ♅
A quick-witted, versatile, adaptable, original and inventive personality is indicated. Freedom of expression and action are important to this person although insufficient rest could lead to some nervous tension.

☉ ☌ ♆
A born romantic, inspirational and idealistic, this individual needs to keep both feet firmly planted on the ground. Usually artistically gifted, such an individual can be unconventional and rather impractical.

☉ ☌ ♇
Tremendous energy and real depth of feeling are indicated. There is a need to understand and respect the wishes and feelings of others otherwise such strong emotions could become misdirected and lead to a power complex.

☉ ☌ Asc
This aspect strongly emphasises the Sun sign. It denotes a sound physical constitution and powerful energies that need constant supervision or the subject may be inclined to become a little egotistical.

☉ ☌ MC
This denotes drive, enthusiasm, ambition, fame or notoriety. Public life, especially politics, is stressed and the subject will make every effort to achieve success in order to win approbation and acclaim.

☽ ☌ ☿
Witty, clever, sensitive and emotional, these individuals are likely to have creative flair, a good imagination and the ability to put their ideas into practice. They may, however, be inclined to allow their emotions to rule their heads.

☽ ☌ ♀
Sociable, sensitive, tactful and affectionate, this subject has natural charm, is popular and likely to succeed at whatever is attempted. He or she should, though, curb any vanity or tendency to self-indulgence, particularly if participating in public life.

☽ ☌ ♂
This denotes independence of spirit – a fighter of causes, determined, mentally alert and energetic. Emotionally moody and impulsive, such a person is likely to have a very positive sex drive and be rather possessive.

☽ ☌ ♃
Business acumen, reliability, integrity and honesty are indicated. This aspect denotes a vocation or career dedicated to helping the less fortunate. Sympathetic to humanitarian ideals, this subject may, however, be inclined to pomposity.

☽ ☌ ♄
A dutiful, loyal, deeply thoughtful personality is indicated. Although such people may be mentally brilliant and well able to assume responsibility, they may be too serious-minded and tend to criticise the inability of others to cope.

☽ ☌ ♅
This aspect can denote rather extreme tendencies – someone who desires personal freedom at any cost. Resourceful, clever and intuitive, such an individual is likely to be rather unconventional, a little eccentric and not always reliable.

☽ ☌ ♆
Emotional and sensitive, intuitive and compassionate, this subject is very impressionable, rather vulnerable and inclined to avoid reality. Often, however, this aspect denotes mediumistic abilities and/or artistic talent.

☽ ☌ ♇
This aspect signifies strong, deep emotions – an impulsive passionate nature. Somewhat erratic and overbearing on occasion, such a person may seek change merely for the sake of change and will be inclined to take unnecessary risks.

☽ ☌ Asc
This conjunction indicates an emotional personality and emphasises the qualities of the rising sign. If from the 1st House, it denotes a restless, changeable nature; from the 12th it signifies an imaginative, idealistic, sentimental temperament.

☽ ☌ MC
Although indicative of a slow starter, once such people set their sights on objectives they could be highly successful, particularly in any form of business partnership. A public career could appeal to these personable, sociable individuals.

☿ ☌ ♀
Persuasive, diplomatic, graceful and charming, these subjects seek harmony in all aspects of their lives. Usually artistically gifted, they may well be able to put their creative talents to practical use in their professional lives.

☿ ☌ ♂
This denotes a quick, perceptive, agile mentality. Such an individual may be argumentative and sententious, but without any malice. A scientific career could appeal to his or her alert mind and natural curiosity, as could journalism or broadcasting.

☿ ☌ ♃
An interest in educational matters is indicated. Just and honest, hard but fair, this subject will earn respect. Intelligent and shrewd in business, he or she can be persistent and stubborn on occasion despite a philosophical attitude.

☿ ☌ ♄
Conscientious and authoritative, this individual is a natural leader. Precise and rather serious-minded, emotions are kept well in check although trust will be repaid by loyalty. A mathematical or scientific ability is likely.

☿ ☌ ♅
Mental originality, brilliance, and perception are the keywords. Objective, intuitive, individualistic and independent, such a person may dislike traditional ideas and will always try something new.

☿ ☌ ♆
Creative and sensitive, but inclined to the sensational, this subject may be over imaginative and too impressionable – a bit of a dreamer. Photography or film-making is likely to appeal, so may clairvoyance or psychicism.

☿ ☌ ♇
Strong will-power, perception and resourcefulness are indicated. Perhaps inclined to use others for their own ends, such people are capable of turning most things to advantage and are likely to succeed in their aims. Occultism may attract their investigative natures.

☿ ☌ Asc
This aspect denotes a high level of intelligence, restlessness and an inclination to loquacity. Logical but dispassionate, such folk make good leaders once they have learned to understand the emotional needs of others.

☿ ☌ MC
Communication is the keyword associated with this conjunction. This mentally alert individual is always ready to assimilate new ideas and facts for future use, to acquire and pass on information, whether through the media or teaching.

☿ ☌ ♂
This aspect signifies a magnetic personality – someone with powerful creative energies, a generally physical nature and strong vitality. Sensitive and easily aroused, such a person is likely to possess plenty of sex appeal.

♀ ☌ ♃
Friendly, optimistic, sympathetic and easy-going, this subject may be a little self-indulgent and inclined to be lazy. A good mediator, this sociable individual's talents are best employed in dealing with other people – especially the opposite sex.

♀ ☌ ♄
A somewhat complex emotional attitude is indicated. Fair-minded, loyal and dutiful, probably with artistic or musical ability, such a person may postpone marriage until later in life when material ambitions have been realised.

♀ ☌ ♅
Emotionally independent, idealistic and unconventional, this individual tends to blow hot and cold in personal relationships. Rather lazy, he or she needs to think before taking action, and to show greater consideration for others.

♀ ☌ ♆
Very impressionable and sensitive, these subjects need to exercise caution otherwise their over-active imaginations could easily lead to deception, disillusionment and impracticality. Artistic pursuits could provide outlets for their fertile imaginations.

♀ ☌ ♇
A romantic, sensual nature is indicated – someone rather too inclined to fall in love with love. The theatre or the arts may appeal to this person's sense of drama although an inherent financial ability could prove useful in business enterprises.

♀ ☌ Asc
In a woman's chart, this aspect denotes physical beauty; in a man's, natural charm. In both cases, the subject is likely to attain influence and respect despite a tendency to lapse into periods of dreamy self-indulgence or narcissism.

♀ ☌ MC
Socially and professionally ambitious, it is easy for these tactful, diplomatic people to achieve their aims. Attracted to careers in public relations or entertainment, they may make successful marriages through business connections.

♂ ☌ ♃
Open, frank and decisive, these subjects have plenty of joie de vivre and money tends to come and go with equal facility. Energetic and forceful, they are natural leaders with magnetic personalities but may be inclined to take too many risks.

♂ ☌ ♄
Inherently strong, resourceful and courageous, such a subject possesses excellent leadership potential. However, he or she may be a little inhibited and, if unable to overcome this trait, could become resentful, envious and malicious.

♂ ☌ ♅
Wilful, intolerant and rebellious, this individual thrives on danger and is attracted to the new or unusual. Temperamentally suited to a mechanical or scientific career, such a person needs constant variety and mental stimulation.

♂ ☌ ♆
This denotes charm and poise but a rather impractical attitude towards emotional relationships, perhaps due to an impressionable nature. Very ambitious, this person is capable of secrecy and ruthlessness in the pursuit of his or her aims.

♂ ☌ ♇
Strong will-power, plenty of physical energy and intense emotions all add up to a somewhat violent temperament. These characteristics may be used constructively or destructively according to mood.

♂ ☌ Asc
Naturally aggressive and with a dominant personality, this individual tends to be impulsive and competitive. Such strong energies need to be well controlled and sensibly directed, particularly as diplomacy may be lacking.

♂ ☌ MC
Extremely ambitious for power and status, these people may be attracted to politics, the armed services or an industrial career. Lively and energetic, they undertake everything with verve and can be passionate about their enthusiasms.

♃ ☌ ♄
Hard-working and conscientious, this serious-minded individual can be patient and persevering in the pursuit of his or her ambitions. Such a person usually has business ability and is able to achieve a reasonable level of success.

♃ ☌ ♅
This denotes a practical, forward-looking personality: a good organiser with innovative talent who is not afraid to experiment. Restless and wilful if thwarted, this person needs to be able to give free rein to his or her self-expression.

♃ ☌ ♆
An idealistic and imaginative temperament is indicated. Although these subjects may tend to over-estimate their abilities, they are likely to have genuine creative or financial flair. Religion, philosophy or the care of people may attract them.

♃ ☌ ♇
Determined to achieve their ambitions, these forceful individuals have good leadership qualities. They have the ability to understand the motives of others and will utilise this knowledge to good effect in seeking their aims.

♃ ☌ Asc
This aspect denotes a self-confident, optimistic person interested in educational, spiritual and philosophical matters, whether as a student or teacher. It can also signify the possibility of weight or health problems.

♃ ☌ MC
Provided that the subject is straightforward and honest, this position will confer success and prominence in business, politics and the public eye. However, success for personal gain or selfish motives may be desired.

♄ ☌ ♅
Ambitious and self-reliant but somewhat temperamental, this individual is likely to have a pronounced interest in scientific matters. Such a person may, however, be very obstinate and will need to develop self-discipline.

♄ ☌ ♆
Some conflict between idealism and materialism is indicated by this conjunction. The outcome will depend largely on the subject's ability, or otherwise, to balance the idealism of Neptune with the practicality of Saturn.

♄ ☌ ♇
Strongly ambitious and rather secretive, these individuals are patient and hard-working. They may, however, experience periods of frustration unless their efforts win the recognition and approbation of others.

♄ ☌ Asc
An austere and reserved nature is indicated, giving rise to difficulties in expressing the true personality, especially in the early years. Yet, despite an inherent shyness, such a person makes a reliable, loyal friend.

♄ ☌ MC
This denotes a single-minded determination to succeed. Such people will have sufficient ambition, self-discipline and application to reach the top but may not retain this position and could suffer a fall from grace.

♅ ☌ ♆
Deeply philosophical, a seeker after truth, this self-willed individual will be attracted to humanitarian principles. Keenly imaginative and with an inventive, original mind, such a sensitive subject will be highly intuitive.

♅ ☌ ♇
Personal freedom is of prime importance to these non-conformist characters with somewhat revolutionary ideas. Potentially good leaders, they should ensure that their influence is used wisely, for constructive rather than destructive purposes.

♅ ☌ Asc
This aspect marks strong individualism and the subject may be a genius or a crank. Original, broad-minded and progressive, such a person is mentally alert, highly intuitive and prone to nervous tension.

♅ ☌ MC
Sudden reversals of fortune are indicated. This liberal-minded, rebellious individual who is attracted to the unknown or the unusual, both in private and public life, could achieve either fame or infamy.

♆ ☌ ♇
Intellectual idealism is signified here. Such a subject is likely to be deeply interested in the occult, philosophy, religion and spiritual matters, perhaps as a student or, more likely, as a proponent.

♆ ☌ Asc
This creative, intuitive and possibly even psychic personality is highly imaginative and could easily lose touch with reality and dream life away. Any artificial stimulant, such as alcohol or drugs, should therefore be avoided.

♆ ☌ MC
Any form of creative or artistic endeavour is favoured by this conjunction. However, the subject is unlikely to be physically robust and should steer clear of secret intrigues that could result in public scandal.

♇ ☌ Asc
Obstinate and very strong-willed, this character can be subtly aggressive and rather obsessive. Somewhat secretive, his or her attitude may be a little aloof and impersonal, even in close relationships, and could alienate others.

♇ ☌ MC
This authoritative individual is a natural leader, whether in politics, business or industry. Ruthless in his search for power, he or she may work for good or evil and could equally well be attracted to science or occultism.

(2) The Oppositions

☉ ☍ ☽

Although this opposition denotes someone who can be quite objective when the need arises, extremes of temperament, restlessness and some stress in close emotional relationships are also indicated. Physical energy, too, is likely to fluctuate.

☉ ☍ ♂

Mentally alert, able and impulsive, this subject will take risks for worthwhile goals. In personal relationships, this aggressive, not always diplomatic individual needs a more conservative partner to achieve a good balance.

☉ ☍ ♃

An expansive, extravagant personality is indicated – a cheerful, good-natured person with a predilection for rather grandiose schemes. Not always practical and perhaps egoistic, he or she does have a shrewd business sense however.

☉ ☍ ♄

A late marriage is indicated for this capable, hard-working, responsible character. Despite inner confidence, this subject presents a rather reserved, cautious image and should learn to overcome inhibitions and relax more.

☉ ☍ ♅

This signifies an unconventional, independent personality with a slightly rebellious streak. Perhaps a bit too impulsive and inclined to take unnecessary risks, such a person needs constant stimulation and the challenge of something new.

☉ ☍ ♆

Naturally diffident, these very sensitive, emotional subjects tend to undervalue themselves and may, on occasion, take refuge in evasion or deception. A more positive, forthright approach is needed therefore especially in personal relationships.

☉ ☍ ♇

Very stubborn, this forceful individual can be overbearing at times, particularly when his or her plans are undermined or opposed in any way. A more cooperative attitude towards others is necessary if conflict is to be avoided.

☉ ☍ Asc

This aspect signifies a need to be with people, to work in a partnership of some kind. Competitive, such a subject requires the company of others in order to express his or her personality fully or will tend to be meddlesome.

☉ ☍ MC
A calm, harmonious environment is essential to this person's peace of mind. Everything will be fine while things go smoothly but any form of upset, expecially in close relationships, will cause a loss of interest.

☽ ☍ ☿
Nervous excitability may lead to emotional confusion unless controlled. Well-meaning, but a bit of a busy-body, this subject lacks direction, a sense of balance, and is inclined to waste time, money and effort.

☽ ☍ ♀
A rather extreme disposition is indicated – emotional hypersensitivity, possessiveness and an inability to compromise. Yet these warm, loving people thrive on companionship. Unwise financial decisions could result in a dramatic change of fortune.

☽ ☍ ♂
Impatient, temperamental and impulsive, such a subject tends to be brusque in speech and manner. Quickly bored by routine and socially unconventional, he or she should avoid excessive behaviour or habits.

☽ ☍ ♃
A lack of discrimination may be a problem with this aspect. Self-indulgent, extravagant, sometimes arrogant and lazy, this individual lives on nervous energy and should try to control his rather strong emotions a little better.

☽ ☍ ♄
Circumspection is the keyword here. Difficulties may arise, especially in close relationships, due to the inability of these subjects to let their feelings surface. They are too easily discouraged and have a rather formal, uncompromising manner.

☽ ☍ ♅
Unpredictable and subject to extreme moodiness, these people have a tendency to make and break friendships for no apparent reason. Wilful and sometimes perverse, they dislike restrictions of any kind and may mistrust the motives of others.

☽ ☍ ♆
This opposition denotes emotional confusion. There is a danger that this gullible personality will allow himself to drift into doubtful situations due to laziness, irresponsibility or a lack of discernment in choosing his associates.

☽ ☍ ♇
Very intense and highly emotional, such a moody subject can be quite overpowering. Personal relationships in particular will suffer unless this

individual learns to control his or her aggressive attitude and rather extreme, changeable nature.

☽ ☍ Asc

Emotionally dependent, the company and companionship of others is essential to these rather over-excitable people. Yet their inability to understand their own motives and reactions can be disruptive and lead to unnecessary misunderstandings.

☽ ☍ MC

Family and domestic attachments are emphasised here. Conventional, perhaps a bit old-fashioned, this subject needs the security of a stable environment. He or she enjoys caring for others but may be a little too possessive.

☿ ☍ ♂

Greater contentment will follow if these over-critical individuals learn to control their irritation. Sometimes sharp-tongued, they are subject to outbursts of temper and need to develop a more balanced, relaxed attitude.

☿ ☍ ♃

An erratic, over-idealistic personality is indicated. Such a person tends to daydream, overplay his hand and can be stubbornly wilful and intransigent if challenged. Not very dependable, much firmer self-discipline is required.

☿ ☍ ♄

Close relationships could be marred by a suspicious, rather narrow-minded, unforgiving attitude. Unnecessarily defensive and unduly pessimistic, this uncompromising individual does not make friends easily and should try to be more outgoing.

☿ ☍ ♅

This aspect signifies a need for constant stimulation. Quite a rebel, this venturesome person loves to stir things up, though not necessarily with malice. Inconsistent, a bit eccentric, he or she can be blunt, tactless and egoistic when bored.

☿ ☍ ♆

Although intuitive, this personality is also naive, a little too sensitive emotionally and can be evasive and not always truthful. Such under-hand manoeuvring can result in failure, especially if financial deals are involved.

☿ ☍ ♇

Clever, astute, but slightly too intense, these individuals may not always see eye to eye with others. They may be forced to take a less serious approach with colleagues and friends or will find themselves under pressure in relationships.

☿ ☍ Asc
Excitable and mentally alert, this subject functions at his best with a partner, someone with whom he can exchange ideas and opinions. Witty and challenging, his mind is never still for long and needs constant stimulation.

☿ ☍ MC
This denotes a very subjective personality – the sort of person who cannot or will not see another's point of view. Argumentative, inclined to take issue whenever he or she feels like it, such an individual should cultivate a more tolerant attitude.

♀ ☍ ♂
Marriage is not favoured by this aspect because the subject is far too sensitive, easily hurt and sexually uncompromising. There will always be conflict in relationships unless this individual is prepared to learn cooperation.

♀ ☍ ♃
Ostentation, vanity and hypocrisy are the watchwords here. Extravagant – emotionally and materially – such an undisciplined person revels in the luxuries of life and can be quite perverse or eccentric in his or her sexual inclinations.

♀ ☍ ♄
These subjects may be lonely due to an inability to convey their emotional needs to others, whether romantic partners or colleagues. Motives are, therefore, likely to be misunderstood and this can lead to problems.

♀ ☍ ♅
Powerfully motivated, but lacking stability, such a person is easily frustrated and led astray. This individual may experience great difficulty in forming worthwhile, romantic attachments that last due to an overriding desire for freedom.

♀ ☍ ♆
This aspect denotes the strong possibility of self-delusion. Impractical, indulgent, lacking clarity and judgement, these exceptionally emotional characters will view things through rose-coloured spectacles, even when they know it is wrong.

♀ ☍ ♇
A very sensual disposition can lead to all sorts of problems for these people. They show poor judgement in their choice of friends and partners, and joint finances could suffer as a result of their impracticality.

♀ ☍ Asc
Good-natured, generous, warm and affectionate, such outgoing personalities function best as part of a team, or in partnership. Upset by any kind of friction, they need the support of others and the security of marriage.

♀ ☍ MC
This signifies a well-balanced individual. Sociable and popular, this subject should get along well with people of all ages. Home-loving and a good host, this person has little or no tension to disturb the equanimity of his or her nature.

♂ ☍ ♃
An extremely restless temperament is indicated. Keen to travel, and with a strong materialistic streak, this selfish, intolerant, opinionated person finds it difficult to sustain any kind of effort for long and rarely completes a project.

♂ ☍ ♄
Ambivalence is the overriding factor. Sometimes resentful, bitter and forceful, at other times calm, controlled and slow to anger – inclined to blow hot and cold – this subject's moods are unpredictable but do not, as a rule, last for long.

♂ ☍ ♅
Emotionally volatile, this impatient individual's reckless behaviour can result in accident or injury. Stubbornly undisciplined, he or she resents the imposition of restrictions, is irritated by trivia and gives vent to his feelings with outbursts of temper.

♂ ☍ ♆
These subjects' apparent self-confidence tends to dissipate when adverse circumstances arise. Thus they may appear two-faced, although this is not a deliberate trait – they are simply not very adaptable and may find it hard to suppress their feelings.

♂ ☍ ♇
Ruthlessly ambitious for power, this individual wants control but cannot tolerate opposition and may experience difficulty in relating to others. Profoundly emotional, there may also be some inner conflict due to sexual repression.

♂ ☍ Asc
Aggressive and competitive, such a forceful personality reacts strongly to slights, whether real or imaginary, which could alienate others. Yet, despite this somewhat defensive attitude, he or she is basically energetic and enthusiastic.

♂ ☍ MC
Quickly bored by routine and rather impatient, the impulsiveness of these individuals could cause problems. Although they are quite wilful, they can be very successful if they curb their rashness and learn to channel their energies correctly.

♃ ☍ ♄
Rather unimaginative, narrow-minded and intolerant, these people lack real emotional warmth. Though they quite frequently become pillars of society, their lack of enthusiasm and optimism can lead to frustration and discontent.

♃ ☍ ♅
Not confident enough, this subject tends to allow himself to be led into unwise schemes and is often left holding the baby. Something of a maverick, such a person does not enjoy much popularity due to his lack of sympathy, diplomacy and tact.

♃ ☍ ♆
Kind-hearted, helpful and charitable, this generous individual is quite altruistic and may be attracted to religious cults. Almost entirely without any practical sense, he or she may be absent-minded and inclined to lose touch with reality.

♃ ☍ ♇
A complete lack of humility makes these people their own worst enemies. Too autocratic, bombastic and selfishly ambitious to have many close friends they may try to use force rather than persuade others into their way of thinking.

♃ ☍ Asc
These folk are always willing to learn from experience or from others. Gregarious, they have numerous friends and acquaintances, perhaps older than themselves, but have a tendency to idolise others and this can lead to disillusionment.

♃ ☍ MC
This aspect places emphasis on domestic issues: the home will represent a safe refuge where the subject can retire to recharge his or her batteries. Although inclined to resent any loss of personal freedom, this person is emotionally well-adjusted.

♄ ☍ ♅
A lack of common sense could create problems for this slightly unstable personality. Sometimes rebellious and dictatorial, this individual's behaviour can be unpredictable despite the fact that he can work hard should the occasion arise.

♄ ☍ ♆
Deception is the danger here. Capable of deceit as well as gullible, such people could end up with nothing unless they are careful. Hopelessly unrealistic, they become involved in impractical schemes and need to come down to earth.

♄ ☍ ♇
Misfortune seems to dog these people. Usually the victims of circumstances beyond their control, even those who attain positions of authority may suffer reversals of fortune. They should, therefore, be very wary in their dealings with others.

♄ ☍ Asc
The emphasis is on maturity. Fair-minded and just, but rather staid and unenterprising, these individuals will admire and respect their elders. They tend to be loners and may not marry until later in life, possibly to partners older than themselves.

♄ ☍ MC
This aspect denotes a self-contained character. Rather prim and proper, such a person may have difficulty in close relationships although he may have a wide circle of acquaintances on a more formal, social level.

♅ ☍ ♆
Confused by that which is not understood, not very practical and inclined to fantasise, these folk experience difficulty in facing up to reality. There is a tendency towards escapism, perhaps through indulgence in drink, drugs and sex.

♅ ☍ ♇
A very changeable nature and life-style are indicated. Temperamentally explosive and with rather extreme views on some subjects, this passionate individual can become fanatical and demanding. As life progresses, tremendous changes are likely.

♅ ☍ Asc
Long-term commitments of any kind will not appeal to this freedom-loving personality. Perhaps a bit eccentric, certainly unpredictable, he or she craves variety and will seek the company of those of like mind.

♅ ☍ MC
Very individualistic and self-centred, these subjects will go their own way in life with little or no regard for the thoughts or feelings of others. Any domestic arrangements will, therefore, have to allow them the license they demand.

♆ ☍ ♇
This is a very rare aspect and denotes tension and emotional stress.

These people are not prepared to make concessions for anybody or anything and this attitude can easily lead to conflict between what is possible and what is desirable.

Ψ ☍ Asc
A little too naive, confusion may arise in relationships due to this subject's lack of understanding of other people's motives. Creatively imaginative, he or she may initiate good business schemes but lack the shrewdness to put them into effect.

Ψ ☍ MC
These extremely sensitive subjects yearn for the guidance and leadership of older people whom they can respect. Sadly, though, they may have difficulty in getting on with their parents and similar authority figures, especially in childhood.

♇ ☍ Asc
Tremendous emotional intensity is signified here. This can cause a great deal of contention, particularly as such folk feel strongly that changes of attitude and behaviour on the part of other people are necessary in order for them to live their lives satisfactorily.

♇ ☍ MC
Childhood experiences may colour the life of this individual and cause deep inner conflict. Perhaps overly ambitious, this complex character may acquire specialised knowledge or skills that can bring fame and recognition.

(3) The Squares

☉ □ ☽
This person's generally objective outlook may be at variance with his or her mental perception and alertness. Such temperamental inconsistencies can give rise to domestic misunderstandings during childhood, or to romantic ones in later years.

☉ □ ♂
A lot of time and effort could be wasted on fruitless enterprises by this irrational, impulsive subject. Self-centred, rather brash and overconfident, this person can be argumentative and stubborn whenever he or she fails to get his own way.

☉ □ ♃
More self-control is needed by these extravagant characters if they are to succeed in their aims. Passionately emphatic about what they consider

to be their rights, they tend to exaggerate, and can be quite vindictive if thwarted.

○ □ ♄

This aspect denotes an industrious personality, but one who will have to create his or her own opportunities. Easily frustrated, yet with the determination and perseverance to pursue objectives to the bitter end, this person functions best independently.

○ □ ♅

Inclined to work in fits and starts, nervous tension could cause some problems for this born romantic with high ideals. An adventurous spirit, liberal and enterprising, his behaviour can be erratic, even eccentric.

○ □ ♆

Impractical idealism is indicated by this aspect. Extremist tendencies are likely, both in actions and reactions, and any form of speculation should be avoided as this unreliable personality can easily be taken for a ride.

○ □ ♇

These dominant, forthright characters have good executive potential but need to learn how to compromise. A sense of frustration could cause their usual self-control to slip and they may display passionate outbursts of temperament on occasion.

○ □ Asc

More self-awareness is required by this resourceful, ambitious subject. Unable to cope with any form of criticism, he or she may give a false impression of insincerity and should learn to develop a more open, relaxed manner.

○ □ MC

Self-assertive and with plenty of initiative, such people may be inclined to think that they know it all. Complacency can, however, lead to severe problems, both in personal and professional relationships.

☽ □ ☿

Too subjective for his or her own good, nervous tension may arise due to an inability to separate emotion from reason. A good conversationalist, expressive and witty, this subject can sometimes be too talkative and find it difficult to keep secrets.

☽ □ ♀

Affectionate and kind-hearted but quite indiscriminate in their friendships, these guileless people are easily imposed upon and careless with cash. Sentimental and rather self-indulgent, they need to exercise greater self-discipline.

☽ □ ♂

Although mentally shrewd, these individuals have little control over their emotions, are temperamental and quickly lose their equilibrium. They cannot tolerate any form of interference and tend to overreact whenever they feel their independence is threatened.

☽ □ ♃

This aspect signifies an expansive personality – extravagant, cheerful and optimistic. Self-indulgent, and with a very happy-go-lucky attitude, this person frequently starts a project well but lacks the staying power to see it through.

☽ □ ♄

Analytical, ambitious and serious, these rather conservative people are very self-sufficient. However, despite their apparent confidence, they may be lonely because they are self-contained and have difficulty in expressing their emotional and physical needs.

☽ □ ♅

Anything new or unusual is likely to appeal to these slightly outrageous characters. Excitable, volatile, very individualistic and rebellious, they are inclined to be too outspoken as a rule although they are basically honest and truthful.

☽ □ ♆

Lack of realism could be a problem here. A romantic, sentimental dreamer with a charming manner, such an ingenious personality is easily hurt and inclined to seek refuge in a world of fantasy and illusion rather than face up to reality.

☽ □ ♇

Forthright in speech and action, this individual grows impatient when things do not go well or too slowly. Emotionally intense, he or she nevertheless makes and breaks friendships without any real compunction, sometimes with dramatic results.

☽ □ Asc

A reluctance to assume responsibility could cause problems. Close relationships in particular may suffer, especially as this tense, withdrawn subject has difficulty in expressing his or her emotions adequately and is not very decisive.

☽ □ MC

This aspect denotes those who allow their hearts to rule their heads, even in business matters. All kinds of difficulties can arise as a result of this trait and they need to learn to keep their strong emotions on a much tighter rein.

☿ □ ♂
Very rash, these people tend to jump to conclusions without due cause and should try to curb their overactive imaginations and tactlessness. They would do better to rely more heavily on their mental acuteness and natural sensitivity.

☿ □ ♃
'Fools rush in where angels fear to tread' seems to sum up the implications of this aspect. Sloppy, not very practical or well organised, this subject is inclined to make errors of judgement and certainly needs to develop a greater respect for authority.

☿ □ ♄
Narrow-minded and bigoted, these subjects are pragmatists, lacking in imagination, and are unwilling to experiment with anything new. Very conservative and rather dull, they tend to worry endlessly and needlessly over unimportant trifles and can be jealous.

☿ □ ♅
Keenly imaginative and with a pronounced sense of humour, these likeable characters are avid for new experiences. They are rather excitable, though, and lack the mental control and stability that their personalities need to achieve a good balance.

☿ □ ♆
A very complex character is indicated. Creative and original, such a person can be a bit of a dreamer and may find it difficult to communicate his ideas and feelings properly. An interest in occultism and mysticism is likely.

☿ □ ♇
Naturally secretive and subtle tacticians, these subjects are also strong-willed and can be quite aggressive in putting their ideas across. Such apparent hostility could mar relationships and they may have few really close friends, so should temper their attitude.

☿ □ Asc
A keen, penetrating wit coupled with a fun-loving temperament could result in this person being too easily side-tracked from important issues. He or she is a real chatterbox who thrives on idle gossip and, although shrewd, tends to lack direction.

☿ □ MC
Mentally restless, these individuals have a low tolerance to boredom and may, in fact, pursue more than one career at any given time. They need greater self-discipline in order to be really successful, though, for they are not very perceptive or profound.

♀ □ ♂

Perhaps lacking finesse, these somewhat extreme personalities should ensure that their physical and emotional desires are not given priority over all other considerations. Unless their passionate natures are correctly channelled, misunderstandings are bound to arise.

♀ □ ♃

Warm-hearted, cheerful and friendly, this subject gets on well with others and is adept at the social graces. He or she is, however, inclined to be self-indulgent, extravagant and a bit lazy, so needs to develop a rather more positive attitude towards life.

♀ □ ♄

An over-cautious nature could create problems of loneliness for these capable, studious people. Although competent, their strong desire for security, peace and quiet makes them too wary in their approach to others and they should try to conquer shyness.

♀ □ ♅

Freedom of expression and action is of the essence to this changeable, unconventional character. Very emotional, such a subject is unreliable and can, therefore, be rather fickle in his or her affections and too easily impressed by superficial attractions.

♀ □ ♆

Emotionally complex, these individuals are inclined to idolise others and, being a rather poor judges of character and motives, could create difficulties for themselves. Their sex lives, in particular, could be unsatisfactory or unconventional.

♀ □ ♇

Passionately intense and very acquisitive, such people will actively seek wealth and material possessions, probably regardless of method. Clever and able to express themselves constructively, these subjects may well have artistic ability.

♀ □ Asc

Good at flattery, the manner of these individuals will win them social popularity. Insincerity may go hand in hand with unreliability, though, because their superficial charm may be deceptive and hide an underlying laziness that could strain relationships.

♀ □ MC

This aspect emphasises the subject's sociability. A genuine liking for company implies that this friendly soul may follow a career that enables him or her to have plenty of contact with others. Any tendency to be over liberal should be curbed, however.

♂ □ ♃

These hasty, impulsive people need to learn moderation. They have great difficulty in keeping their extremist tendencies in check for very long, are inclined to run unnecessary risks much of the time and are easily provoked into senseless actions.

♂ □ ♄

Poor judgement and missed opportunities could lead to frustration for this ambitious subject. Although likely to have executive potential, this person is equally likely to over-estimate his or her own worth and could, therefore, fail to achieve objectives.

♂ □ ♅

Recklessness is the keyword here. A total lack of caution and common sense could lead to enormous problems for these rash, quick-tempered, independent but highly idealistic individuals who never seem able to relax properly.

♂ □ ♆

An ambiguous nature is indicated by this aspect. Emotional and sexual feelings may sometimes be repressed, at other times totally unrestrained. Muddled thinking or unusual beliefs could cause such subjects to seesaw from one extreme to the other.

♂ □ ♇

Extremely ambitious and assertive, no one could doubt the strength of the will-power of these subjects. They should learn to curb their dictatorial attitude, especially as they may be inclined to bend the rules in order to achieve their aims if they feel this is necessary.

♂ □ Asc

This enthusiastic, competitive individual tends to grow impatient when confronted with the negativity of others. He may then make over-hasty decisions, be too forthright in speech and would do well to develop a more tactful, diplomatic approach.

♂ □ MC

Independent, impulsive and a bit mistrustful of others, this subject challenges everything and everyone, almost without thought. Such a contentious attitude can strain relationships – personal, social or professional – so more moderation is needed.

♃ □ ♄

This conservative person could become too hide-bound by convention and lead a rather dull, monotonous life. Perhaps overly concerned with material considerations, he could overreach himself and lose everything as a result of poor planning.

♃ □ ♅
Very liberal and restless, such an independent subject is attracted to impractical schemes and Bohemian behaviour. Extremely impulsive and not always reliable, often he will take on more than he can deliver, sometimes knowingly, sometimes not.

♃ □ ♆
Although they can be smooth and shrewd operators, these folk have a tendency to be indolent on occasion. They are always willing to try out new ideas but are rather gullible, so should rely more on their natural intuition and heed their hunches.

♃ □ ♇
Proud and wilful, these ambitious individuals can be dogmatic and controversial. Such people can get quite carried away by an idea and need to keep their feet firmly on the ground. A less rebellious, more tolerant attitude would be helpful, too.

♃ □ Asc
Often, this aspect signifies that the subject will have success in middle age or later life. Rather prone to expansive, even grandiose schemes, this person could be inclined to use others for his or her own ends and may be somewhat autocratic on occasions.

♃ □ MC
These energetic, versatile characters have wide-ranging interests and are capable of great compassion for the less fortunate. They can be unrealistic about their business abilities yet, with a little common sense and humility, make good bosses.

♄ □ ♅
Inner tensions and inconsistency of temperament and philosophy can cause a changeable attitude and result in surprising alterations to career and life-style. Naturally rebellious but shrewd, such a person's actions are liable to seem irrational.

♄ □ ♆
A basically unstable personality is indicated. Perhaps cunning or devious, possibly dogmatic about beliefs, genuine neuroses could develop. Certainly others are likely to be alienated by his or her self-pitying manner arising from inner fears and confused thinking.

♄ □ ♇
Ruthless ambition and an uncompromising attitude could mar this subject's relationships of all kinds. Power may be sought without compunction or compassion and it would be advisable for this person to be a little more flexible and subtle.

♄ □ Asc
Self-critical and exacting, this individual may well make a rod for his own back. Domestic and close ties could suffer as a result of an impersonal approach and business relationships, too, are unlikely to benefit from such a lack of responsiveness.

♄ □ MC
This square denotes a serious, industrious, but rather reserved personality. A bit too inclined to take on unwelcome responsibilities, such a person should not allow parental domination or family demands to inhibit personal happiness and development.

♅ □ ♆
Inner tension can cause problems for these highly-strung, nervous individuals. Wilful and somewhat set in their ideas and opinions, they feel uneasy and confused if the pattern of their lives are disrupted and have difficulty coping with changing circumstances.

♅ □ ♇
A genuine lack of emotional security and a strong social awareness lie behind this subject's reformist tendencies. In some cases, rebelliousness and eccentricity may manifest; extreme attitudes could cause personal or sexual problems.

♅ □ Asc
These highly independent people have an unhappy knack of upsetting those close to them by demanding total freedom at all times. This trait needs to be tempered, or their marital, personal and business relationships will suffer.

♅ □ MC
This aspect marks true non-conformists – people who resent all forms of discipline and authority and who will frequently flout the rules to suit themselves. Lovers of innovation, they constantly seek change, variety and fresh experiences.

♆ □ ♇
Forceful idealism pervades the whole character of this individual. Attracted to the strange and unusual, such a person may be caught up, perhaps unwittingly, in practices that are not entirely legal or moral. Strong intuitive powers are likely.

♆ □ Asc
Idealistic but unrealistic, these folk have a strong need to come down to earth! Their unreliability and susceptibility lead to many misunderstandings, particularly in personal relationships, and they should learn to exercise stronger self-discipline.

Ψ □ MC
Lazy and disorganised, this subject's apparent irresponsibility stems from an innate insecurity. Naturally shy and reserved, such a person's negative characteristics can be overcome by sensible guidance from perceptive parents or teachers in early life.

♇ □ Asc
This individual's dictatorial and domineering attitude causes resentment and can mar close personal relationships. Intense and secretive, he or she is nonetheless often successful in business where aggressive competitiveness is not so misplaced.

♇ □ MC
Determination is the overriding characteristic here. Often motivated by a strong desire to change the system and impose his or her methods on others, such a person is rarely content to take a back seat and can be disruptive and overbearing.

(4) The Trines

○ △ ☽
This trine denotes a nicely balanced personality. Sociable and emotionally stable, relationships are likely to be smooth and easy for such a well-adjusted individual. Usually fond of children, he or she has the vitality and temperament necessary to get on well with them.

○ △ ♂
Competent and confident, energetic and enthusiastic, this subject enjoys a challenge and may well be attracted to sports and physical activities that test strength and stamina. Honest and straightforward, his or her drive and integrity earn respect.

○ △ ♃
A sunny disposition is indicated – optimistic, creative and generous. Usually successful and easy-going, these folk tend to let things coast along and only make an effort to bring their undoubted talents into play when it proves absolutely necessary.

○ △ ♄
Quietly competent, these people have good organisational ability and will achieve their aims through sheer hard work and dedication. Careful, cautious and considerate, they are emotionally stable and tend to make friends with those older than themselves.

☉ △ ♅

Sometimes known as the astrologer's aspect, this configuration denotes a life of change and variety. Humane, progressive and original, this magnetic personality has an investigative nature and is ever seeking fresh experiences.

☉ △ ♆

Rather sensitive to people and atmosphere, such intuitive, emotional subjects may be drawn towards the arts. Their cultural and social sense is strong and they have a happy knack of doing and saying the right things at the right time.

☉ △ ♇

Tremendous energy is indicated here. Although well able to take changes in their stride, they dislike confused thinking or indirect methods, and can be rather extreme in the pursuance of objectives because they are inclined to ignore the advice or opinions of others.

☉ △ Asc

Self-confident, positive and talented, these people are particularly suited to work that involves the public. Generally able to win the cooperation of others, this trait plus a magnanimous nature implies that marriage and other partnerships will thrive.

☉ △ MC

Early success is marked by this trine. Practical, strongly idealistic and with plenty of self-confidence and drive, such subjects are very ambitious yet have the qualities necessary to achieve their aims and gain public prominence and acclaim.

☽ △ ☿

Common sense is the keyword here. A good memory and fluency of expression may lead the subject to pursue a career in the communications industry although his or her creative talents may be put to use in a more practical, physical manner as a craftsman, for instance.

☽ △ ♀

This aspect denotes a charming disposition which enhances the feminine attributes of kindness, gentleness and consideration. Often artistically inclined and perhaps just a little lazy, such a warm, affectionate person has a soothing effect on others.

☽ △ ♂

Energetic and enterprising, these exuberant personalities have good leadership qualities although they may not always choose to exercise them. Clever and practical, they have the strength of purpose and ability to achieve their objectives.

☽ △ ♃
Honesty, integrity and openness are indicated. Industrious yet imaginative, such folk will work hard and cheerfully to obtain a satisfactory level of material comfort although they are too altruistic and selfless to be truly ambitious.

☽ △ ♄
Sincere, shy, reserved and somewhat conservative, these subjects possess plenty of common sense. They take their responsibilities seriously, work steadily towards their goals, are practical and often display a certain degree of business acumen.

☽ △ ♅
Vivacious, energetic and optimistic, these outgoing individuals are innovative, imaginative and always seeking the new and unusual. Cheerful and good-natured, they dislike restrictions of any kind and their lifestyle is likely to be unconventional.

☽ △ ♆
A fertile imagination plus good artistic appreciation and ability are indicated. Intuitive, perhaps interested in psychic matters, the subject may be a little over-sensitive and inclined to be rather too emotional on occasion despite an underlying selflessness.

☽ △ ♇
These intensely emotional people can be rather introspective yet are strong-willed enough to keep their feelings firmly in check. They have a lively curiosity, are attracted to the off-beat, but have the sight and determination to overcome any obstacles.

☽ △ Asc
Sensitive and highly emotional, these sociable people often have a playful sense of humour and make delightful companions and partners. Imaginative and creative, they usually have the skills necessary to put their talents to constructive use.

☽ △ MC
Practical and sensible, these subjects are likely to be successful in both personal and professional life due to their innate ability to get on well with others. Emotionally sensitive and very adaptable, they are temperamentally suited to public careers.

☿ △ ♂
Clever, imaginative and mentally alert, these folk need constant intellectual stimulation. Honest and truthful, but not always tactful, they need to learn how to channel their mental energies constructively or will feel restless and dissatisfied.

☿ △ ♃
Good planning and organisational abilities are marked by this trine. Self-assured and articulate, such people may be attracted to educational pursuits and are likely to travel extensively in order to broaden their outlook and add to their store of knowledge.

☿ △ ♄
Mental astuteness and manual dexterity are the key qualities here. Science, mathematics, accountancy or any work requiring precision, patience and practicality is likely to appeal to this logical, methodical and financially shrewd individual.

☿ △ ♅
An enquiring mind and insatiable curiosity could lead this very lively, independent character to investigate many unorthodox subjects. Broad-minded, creative, intuitive and innovative, such a person has an innate understanding and sympathy for people.

☿ △ ♆
Highly imaginative and intuitive, these subjects may be attracted to the visual arts and are sufficiently subtle in their approach to be successful. Although capable and industrious, they may lack persistence and need greater self-discipline.

☿ △ ♇
Serious-minded and intense, such people have a strong social sense and will not tolerate any form of injustice. Practical and realistic in their attitude to everyday affairs, they are also interested in broader issues.

☿ △ Asc
Quick-witted, intelligent and perceptive, these folk can express themselves fluently and easily win the cooperation of others. Able to present and implement their ideas, they are also practical and enjoy learning.

☿ △ MC
Intellectually inclined and mentally alert, these subjects make good teachers and instructors because they are able to communicate well and have warm, friendly dispositions. Hard-working, they are persevering in the pursuit of their ambitions.

♀ △ ♂
A fun-loving, sociable personality is indicated. Energetic and emotionally sensitive, the subject has a strong sex appeal and drive. Enthusiastic and creative, though may not necessarily be artistic.

♀ △ ♃
Warm, affectionate and sympathetic, these folk willingly help those less fortunate than themselves and many enter the service industries. They

like harmonious surroundings and relationships and their friendly, easy-going natures endear them to others.

♀ △ ♄
Emotionally well-adjusted but rather reserved, these individuals are very loyal to their friends and beliefs. Sensible, practical and industrious, they usually have sound business sense and may be artistically or musically inclined.

♀ △ ♅
This trine denotes a vivacious personality. Sunny, sociable and entertaining, the performing arts are likely to appeal to such a spontaneous character whose obvious optimism and joy for life make him or her a lively, exciting companion.

♀ △ ♆
These warm, affectionate, kindly folk are very sympathetic and understanding – especially towards the needy or unfortunate – but may not be practical. Impressionable and idealistic, they may be religiously inclined.

♀ △ ♇
This aspect denotes a deeply emotional nature and a very positive sex drive. Close relationships are, therefore, important to such a person although he or she has little time for boring activities or people who will not make an effort to help themselves.

♀ △ Asc
Women are favoured by this trine because it signifies the feminine attributes of beauty and charm. Friendly, warm and affectionate, other people naturally seek this attractive person's company. Such subjects are creative, so an artistic career is likely.

♀ △ MC
Happy-go-lucky and sociable, this subject appreciates beautiful, harmonious surroundings and is artistically inclined. Amiable, yet professionally ambitious, such a persuasive character is well suited to a career involving direct public contact or as an entertainer.

♂ △ ♃
Energetic, enthusiastic and humane, these freedom-loving individuals like to be with and work with people. Positive and constructive, they will work hard to achieve their ambitions and to help others and are very frequently successful.

♂ △ ♄
Practical, shrewd and ambitious, this subject has the confidence and strength of purpose necessary to succeed. Very industrious, he or she

takes responsibilities seriously and has the ability to grasp any opportunities that arise and use them constructively.

♂ △ ♅

Strong-willed, independent and resourceful, such people have plenty of initiative and drive but are, perhaps, rather inclined to lose interest quickly and to seek new challenges. Practical, inventive and clever with their hands, they may have mechanical skills.

♂ △ ♆

This trine denotes acute perception and sensitivity. Warm and affectionate but a little shy, this attractive personality has strong intuitive powers and the ability to put them to practical use in business and personal life.

♂ △ ♇

Ambitious, decisive and constructive, these dynamic individuals can be quite formidable if opposed. Very strong-willed, with great stamina, they usually have resilient constitutions and will fight hard to overcome any obstacles in their way.

♂ △ Asc

A very positive nature is indicated. Independent, forceful and ambitious, though not always tactful, such subjects have very firm beliefs and ideals. Physically active, outdoor activities or sports will attract.

♂ △ MC

Confident and hard-working, these ambitious folk have the determination necessary to achieve the status and security they desire. Energetic and tenacious, they are likely to achieve prominence in their chosen fields and many gain positions of power.

♃ △ ♄

This configuration marks executive ability – someone with sound business sense who can delegate, make decisions and implement large-scale plans with ease. Responsible and sincere, such a person takes obligations seriously and would do well in a public career.

♃ △ ♅

An interest in the humanities and in social reform could lead this individual to enter politics. Progressive and optimistic, he dislikes restrictions of any sort, has good leadership qualities and is able to turn opportunities to advantage.

♃ △ ♆

Profoundly idealistic, these generous, hospitable characters are not always practical enough to implement their charitable impulses. Yet they are intuitive, perhaps psychic, can inspire others with their enthusiasm and may have healing powers.

♃ △ ♇
Very high moral standards are indicated. A social reformer, honourable, ethical and peace-loving, such a person is inclined to be a little too serious although he or she possesses an instinctive insight into and understanding of human frailty.

♃ △ Asc
Social adaptability and an ability to win the cooperation of others enable this individual to achieve popularity and emotional harmony. Good-humoured, optimistic and gregarious, he or she has an enquiring mind and loves to investigate anything new or unusual.

♃ MC
This trine is the hallmark of professional success. Honest, sincere and competent, these subjects earn the respect and confidence of influential people who can promote their chosen careers and their material success enables them to provide well for their families.

♄ △ ♅
A constructive attitude and an interest in understanding the motivations of others and the self point to astrological or other forms of counselling as a career. Innovative, practical and strong-willed, organisational and executive abilities are stressed.

♄ △ ♆
Financially astute, with managerial potential, these realistic folk mature early and are very serious-minded. Analytical, good at finding and evaluating facts, they are particularly well suited to investigate work.

♄ △ ♇
These profound characters have the ability to learn by their mistakes; they may prefer their own company to that of others and can be relentless in the pursuit of their goals. An interest in the occult – both practical and theoretical – is likely.

♄ △ Asc
A little too cautious and reserved, these people need to learn to relax and enjoy the pleasures of life more. Yet, despite their apparent indifference and reluctance to display emotion, they are warm, sensitive and loyal.

♄ △ MC
Reliable, honest and sincere, this subject is very industrious. But such a controlled, conservative personality can become too detached from the normal social niceties and emotional relationships will suffer unless a conscious effort is made to counteract this trait.

♅ △ ♆
This configuration denotes an active interest in the occult, mysticism,

astrology and related subjects. Such a person is perceptive, and has a charming manner but may be rather inclined to jump to conclusions.

♅ △ ♇

Very strong-willed and far too idealistic, these folk are intent on reforming society although their attitudes tend to change as they grow older. The occult will attract, though there is a danger that their compulsive natures could outweigh common sense.

♅ △ Asc

A magnetic personality is indicated by this trine. Purposeful, and insatiably curious, this person has a bright, infectious manner, good leadership qualities, a degree of intuition and is able to instil others with enthusiasm and optimism.

♅ △ MC

Highly individualistic, these people are creative, inventive and innovative and may choose unusual careers. Professional success is likely to come their way, perhaps associated with fame or, if negatively expressed, infamy or notoriety.

♆ △ ♇

This trine is indicative of a pronounced interest in metaphysical subjects, particularly reincarnation and life after death. This individual may hold unusual views or ascribe to strange philosophies which, in a weak personality, can lead to self-deception.

♆ △ Asc

Imaginative, creative, idealistic, and intuitive, this subject is likely to be psychically talented. A sensitive, sympathetic nature plus an articulate, sociable manner enhance this person's attractiveness and win friendship.

♆ △ MC

An unusual ability to communicate well on all levels is indicated by this aspect. Able to use their intuition constructively, such people benefit from their relationships and are likely to gain public recognition.

♇ △ Asc

Able to initiate and implement great changes to their environment, these progressive characters have reformist tendencies. Determined, and with excellent powers of concentration, they may be attracted to work of an investigative or scientific nature.

♇ △ MC

A driving ambition to succeed is the overriding factor here. This subject has a very acquisitive nature – for facts as well as material possessions – a good executive ability and easily wins the cooperation of those who can help him achieve his aims.

CHAPTER 7
Signs, Parts and Special Planetary Emphasis

Sign classification

The signs of the zodiac are divided into different classifications. Primarily, they are classified as masculine or feminine, positive or negative.

The masculine or positive signs are Aries, Gemini, Leo, Libra, Sagittarius and Aquarius; the feminine or negative signs are Taurus, Cancer, Virgo, Scorpio, Capricorn and Pisces. The masculine/positive signs are considered to be more outgoing, more forward looking than the feminine/negative signs.

The zodiacal signs also fall into groups of Triplicities or elements: Fire, Earth, Air and Water, each of which is credited with particular characteristics.

The Fire signs:
Aries, Leo and Sagittarius are self-sufficient and individualistic. Their nature is positive; they are energetic and enthusiastic, ardent, expressive and vital.

The Earth signs:
Taurus, Virgo and Capricorn are all practical, critical and tend by nature to be negative. They are also methodical and concerned with physical, concrete expression.

The Air signs:
Gemini, Libra and Aquarius are positive and intellectual by nature. Adaptable but not always practical, communication is their forte and they always want to improve everything.

The Water signs:
Cancer, Scorpio and Pisces are negative. Their nature is emotional; they are sensual, impressionable and creative. They make good managers and understand the problems of others.

A further subdivision is the Quadruplicities: Cardinal, Fixed and Mutable. These, too, have special qualities.

The Cardinal signs:
Aries, Cancer, Libra and Capricorn fall in this category. Their overall quality is one of action. Constructive and assertive, spontaneous, opportunistic and ambitious, they express themselves quite enthusiastically.

The Fixed signs:
Taurus, Leo, Scorpio and Aquarius are Fixed signs. The overall quality is tenacity. Persistent and cautious, steady and reliable, slow but sure, they possess good powers of concentration.

The Mutable signs:
Gemini, Virgo, Sagittarius and Pisces are Mutable. Their overall quality is flexibility. Adaptable, practical but sentimental, indecisive and superficial, they blend in with their environment.

Planetary dignities

By sign and by house position the planets take on different effects according to where they are found. These relative strengths and weaknesses, or planetary dignities as they are called, are Rulership, Exaltation, Detriment and Fall.

Each planet *rules* a sign and has additional emphasis *(exaltation)* in others. They are also considered to have a poor effect *(detriment)* in some signs or virtually no effect *(fall)* in certain others.

Planets in certain houses may show additional strengths or weaknesses because they correspond with sign positions 'by accident'. (A complete table of planetary dignities, including accidental dignities [house position references], is on *page 119*.

At one time, for example, Jupiter was considered to rule Pisces and therefore to be in detriment in Virgo. Thus, in Jean's birth chart, Jupiter could be considered to be in rulership but, at the same time, 'accidentally' in detriment because the 6th House refers to the sign of Virgo, and Virgo would be detrimental to the power of Jupiter. So, we have a curious situation where a planet can be regarded as strong and weak at the same time.

Rising planet

A planet in the Ascendant, that is within 7° of the cusp of the 1st House, may be termed the rising planet and has special emphasis. In some charts there may be several planets to choose from and you will have to learn to select the correct, or most influential one from the information available.

Sign Classifications

Sign	Symbol	Polarity	Quadruplicity	Triplicity or Element
Aries	♈	+	Cardinal	Fire
Taurus	♉	−	Fixed	Earth
Gemini	♊	+	Mutable	Air
Cancer	♋	−	Cardinal	Water
Leo	♌	+	Fixed	Fire
Virgo	♍	−	Mutable	Earth
Libra	♎	+	Cardinal	Air
Scorpio	♏	−	Fixed	Water
Sagittarius	♐	+	Mutable	Fire
Capricorn	♑	−	Cardinal	Earth
Aquarius	♒	+	Fixed	Air
Pisces	♓	−	Mutable	Water

In Jean's chart, however, the Moon is the only choice, even though it is 8° away from the 1st House cusp. If, though, Saturn had been at 17° Virgo instead of 2° Libra, then this would have been the rising planet in Jean's chart.

The rising planet helps to colour the psychology of the character. In Jean's case, the Moon's influence means that she will regard new acquaintances with inner wariness and adapt to them slowly, irrespective of any outer display of friendliness or acceptance that she may make.

The Midheaven

When using the Equal House system, the Midheaven (usually written as MC for short) rarely falls exactly on the 9th/10th House cusp and its position is therefore normally indicated between the two outer circles of the chart wheel.

The Midheaven provides a clue to the subject's likely career, profession or vocation according to the sign quality and element involved. In

Jean's chart the Midheaven is at 10° Gemini: a sign which signifies communication and implies intellectual alertness. So Jean would need a job that kept her mentally stimulated and, preferably, where she had contact with other people.

As another example, Capricorn on the MC would imply that the subject was professionally ambitious, patient and possessed managerial abilities. Always look to see where the ruler of the MC is in a chart because this will furnish a clue as to which area of his life the subject would like to emphasise should his career prove successful.

Arabic Parts

The Arabic Parts are little used in astrology nowadays although at one time a hundred or more of these Parts or Points were in regular use. They have fascinating names, a rather nebulous history and were considered to have specific influences upon the life of the subject according to their positions in a chart.

They are sensitive points in a chart and can, in certain circumstances, have a bearing on the personality of the subject whose chart is under consideration. One of these Parts, the Part of Fortune (or Fortuna) is still used by some astrologers who consider it to be an indication of material good fortune relating to those matters pertaining to the house in which it is placed.

The formula for finding the Part of Fortune's position in a chart is: Ascendant plus Moon minus Sun. This is calculated by expressing the zodiacal longitude of these points as figures and simply completing the sum. Again, we will use Jean's chart as our example:

Ascendant 15° Virgo (i.e. 150°+15°) = 165
plus Moon 23° Virgo (i.e. 150°+23°) = 173
338
minus Sun 9° Capricorn (i.e. 270°+9°)
= 279
59

59° equates to 29° Taurus

So, in Jean's chart the Part of Fortune is at 29° Taurus, and the symbol for this Part (⊗) would be entered in the 9th House, close to the centre of the chart and in different coloured ink from the planets so that it is easy to recognise.

In some charts the combined longitude of the Moon and Ascendant may be less than that of the Sun. In such instances 360 is added to the sum; similarly, if the total is more than 360° then 360 is deducted.

The Nodes of the Moon

The nodes are the two points at which the orbit of the Moon intercepts the ecliptic as it travels from the North to the South latitude and back again. The position of the Moon's north node (☊) is always listed in the ephemeris and the position of the south node (☋) is exactly opposite this point. For example, in Jean's chart the north node is at 23° Pisces in the 7th House, so the south node's position is opposite – 23° Virgo in the 1st House.

As the nodes are exactly opposite one another, often only the north node's position is entered in a chart. Again, it is useful to place the symbol near the centre of the wheel in a different coloured ink.

There are considerable differences of opinion regarding their exact interpretation although, in general, the north node is regarded as beneficial and the south as indicative of possible losses. Also, if found on or near the Ascendant/Descendant line, the nodes could have a bearing on the physical appearance of the subject – unusual height say.

Fixed stars

The term 'fixed star' is misleading because all the heavenly bodies do, in fact, move. It is simply that the fixed stars of ancient astrology move very slowly indeed, perhaps only 50 seconds a year! Although there are over a hundred of these bodies listed, all of which have meanings ascribed to them, they are little used today although they can, occasionally, provide an explanation for sudden unexpected events for which there is no other apparent reason in a chart. They are more often used in horary astrology than in natal astrology.

Midpoints

In very simple terms, midpoints are exactly what their name implies: they are the midway points between any two other sensitive points in a chart, whether these are planets, the Ascendant, MC, or whatever.

Most midpoints are not marked by another planet of significant point but are merely sensitive points which can be triggered off by transits, progressions, etc. and they are beyond the scope of this book.

However, here is an example of how to calculate a midpoint. If, for instance, Mars is at 1° Aries and Venus at 1° Cancer, these two planets would be 90° apart. Half of this is 45°, so the midway point between these two planets would fall on 15° Taurus.

Asteroids

In recent years there has been a marked interest in the study of asteroids and their possible influence on a chart, partly on the principle that they may well be the exploded remains of what was once a planet. However, although some of the written material available on this subject may be valid, some of the asteroids so vividly described are theoretical rather than actual, so the whole subject should be approached with caution.

Chiron, Ceres, Pallas, Juno and Vesta do at least physically exist, so you could test the validity of their influence in your own chart or those of people well-known to you; always be prepared to experiment, but do not be too ready to jump to conclusions.

Retrograde planets

At certain times a planet (or planets) may appear to be moving backwards – contrary to the general direction of the planets in the Solar system – when viewed from the Earth. When this happens, the planet concerned is said to be retrograde and the symbol R_e is used to denote this apparent motion.

When erecting a chart it is important to note any retrograde planets and to mark them as such in the chart. Although there are strong differences of opinion between astrologers concerning the significance of retrogradation, it is generally considered to retard or withhold the gifts or qualities with which the planet concerned is associated. If this is so, this difference of effect will be more marked when a retrograde planet turns direct by progression.

The opposite of retrograde (R_e) is direct (D), and these apparent changes of direction by a planet are always indicated in ephemerides by the symbols shown in brackets against the dates when they occur. A planet that is changing from one direction to the other is, of course, temporarily stationary (STAT); if stationary and about to move along its normal orbit, it is stationary direct (SD); and when stationary but about to retrograde, it is described as stationary retrograde (SR).

A stationary planet is regarded by some astrologers as having extra emphasis because it is, by staying in one place, radiating more energy than if it were moving. However, as stated, opinions vary considerably concerning the whole subject of retrogradation although it has more significance when transits or progressions are being used.

Special Planetary Emphasis

A birth chart is divided into different segments – houses, quadrants and hemispheres – and not infrequently there will be more planets in one particular section than in the others. The significance of any such planetary emphasis must, of course, be taken into consideration when judging the horoscope as a whole, so here are brief guidelines to help you.

Firstly though, it is important to familiarise yourself with the 'angles' which are used to divide a chart into the various sections and these are: the Ascendant, Midheaven (MC or *Medium Coeli*), Descendant and Nadir (IC or *Immum Coeli*). These sensitive points in a chart correspond to the East, South, West and North respectively, although, as a natal chart is a symbolic map of the heavens for the moment of birth as viewed from the place of birth (i.e. the Earth), the compass points appear to be in the wrong quarters. *(See page 6).*

Angular, Succedent and Cadent
Traditionally, the houses in a chart were designated as Angular, Succedent and Cadent; the first category being regarded as 'strongest' and the third as 'weakest'. However, most modern astrologers consider the houses to have equal weight and, therefore, prefer to classify them as Cardinal, Fixed and Mutable. (In any case, if using the Equal House system, the MC may not fall on the 10th House cusp, so such house classifications would not be strictly accurate.)

So, Houses 1, 4, 7 and 10 can be designated as Angular or Cardinal and a majority of planets in these houses would emphasise the qualities associated with Cardinal signs – initiation, action and leadership.

Houses 2, 5, 8 and 11 are Succedent and correlate to the Fixed signs. A majority of planets here would emphasise activities of a consolidating nature – perseverence, determination and will-power.

Houses 3, 6, 9 and 12 are Cadent and correspond to the Mutable signs. A planetary emphasis here would accentuate the quality of flexibility, implying mental activity and adaptability.

Quadrants
The Ascendant/Descendant axis (or horizon, as it is known) and the MC/IC axis divide a chart into four quadrants and four hemispheres, each of which may be emphasised in some way by the distribution of planets in the chart.

For instance, four or more planets in the first quadrant – Houses 1, 2 and 3 – imply that the subject will want to experience things at first-hand. Initiative will be marked and the character will be either selfless or selfish because everything will be pursued at a very personal level.

A grouping of planets in the second quadrant – Houses 4, 5 and 6 – indicates a subjective nature: someone who may be content to remain in the background and allow others to take the lead. The home and domestic affairs are likely to dominate such a person's life.

A planetary emphasis in the third quadrant – Houses 7, 8 and 9 –

signifies an objective awareness of others. Likely to put the needs of other people before their own, such subjects are sociable and usually enjoy harmonious, successful partnerships.

When the fourth quadrant – Houses 10, 11 and 12 – is emphasised, it stresses responsibility. Social standing and obligations will be important to the subject who is likely to be very ambitious.

Hemispheres

If a majority of planets in a chart fall above the horizon (Houses 7-12) the more extrovert aspects of the personality are highlighted. Self-expression is marked and the native is likely to enter public service, politics or any career that deals directly with and depends on the approbation of others. Advancement is usually achieved through the good offices of those in authority, often without soliciting such help.

When the majority of the planets are below the horizon (Houses 1-6) the whole character is much more introspective. Such people are not easy to get to know and may be even more difficult to understand. They can be cautious, reserved and shy; in order to succeed they must work by their own efforts because they rarely receive assistance from those with influence.

If the planetary emphasis falls in the Eastern hemisphere – Houses 10, 11, 12, 1, 2 and 3 – it highlights initiative. Individualism is stressed and the subject is likely to be a self-starter, someone who will initiate ideas and actions. Leadership qualities will be apparent, although the subject's underlying motives may be selfish and egotistic and there could be a tendency to use others for his or her own ends.

A planetary emphasis in the Western hemisphere (Houses 4-9) accentuates the subject's concern with those matters that are outside the self. It focuses attention on emotions, relationships and the native's attitudes towards others, his environment and career. Social awareness and humanitarian tendencies are likely to dominate such a subject's personality.

Chart patterns

Some astrologers use another method of assessing the implications of the way in which planets are distributed in a chart. This method classifies charts into seven different 'types' to describe the 'patterns' made by the planets: the Bundle, Bowl, Bucket, Locomotive, See-saw, Splash and Splay.

The Bundle is used to describe a chart where the planets are grouped closely, occupying only a small section of the zodiac. It therefore points to the specialist, someone who will be concerned with one particular aspect of life and tend to function within specific confines.

The Bowl is similar to the Bundle although the planets are not so tightly grouped and occupy a larger area of the zodiac. It implies a self-contained personality, someone who will absorb experiences. The 'leading' planet will have special significance in such a chart.

The Bucket chart is like the Bowl, but with a 'handle'. Nine planets occupy one hemisphere and the tenth planet is the only one in the other hemisphere. This points to a singularity of purpose; the single planet may indicate the area towards which efforts will be directed.

The Locomotive describes a chart where the planets are fairly evenly distributed except for two or three consecutive houses. Drive and energy

Classification of birth charts according to the planetary distribution pattern

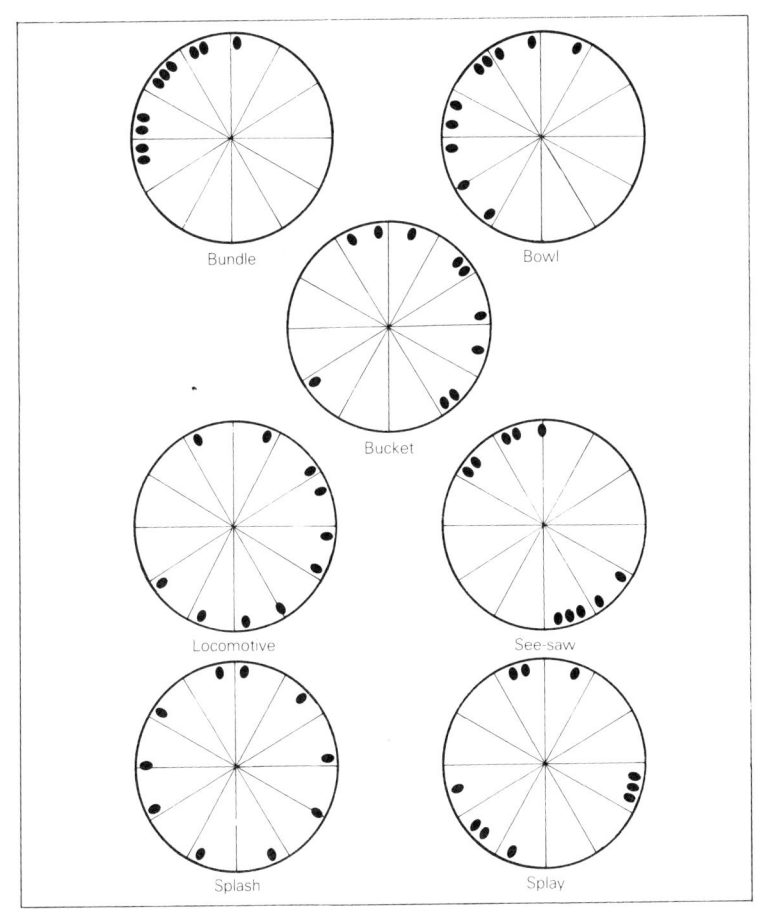

Bundle Bowl

Bucket

Locomotive See-saw

Splash Splay

are the characteristics associated with this pattern; the 'lead' planet and its house position are of particular importance.

The See-saw configuration is one where the planets form two opposing groups, each of which occupies no more than three signs or 90°. This pattern accentuates the two opposing sides of the subject's nature and may indicate conflict or vacillation depending on the planets and signs involved.

The Splash describes a chart where the planets are distributed very evenly, occupying as many signs as possible. In a positive chart it implies a wide range of interests and knowledge; in a negative one it indicates a scattering of energies and lack of direction.

The Splay chart contains at least one stellium (small group of planets) and the planets are, therefore, less evenly distributed than in the splash. Such a configuration signifies the individualist, someone who will resent restrictions or limitations of any kind.

Aspect patterns

Sometimes planets are so positioned in a chart that they form a group of relationships and their aspects form one of the three basic patterns: Tee-Square, Grand Tine or Grand Cross. The Tee-Square is the most common of these and the Grand Cross the rarest.

Tee-Square
This is formed when two planets are in opposition and a third planet, halfway between them, is square to both. Such a configuration can be obstructive and indicate tension unless a fourth planet is in favourable aspect to one of the three involved and so act as an energising factor.

Grand Cross
A Grand Cross is formed when four planets are in square aspect to each other. Thus it indicates a chart which, by definition, must contain at least four squares and two oppositions. The chart accentuates these aspects and it can be regarded as a 'make or break' configuration.

Grand Trine
A Grand Trine is formed when three planets are in trine aspect to each other. It may therefore form a triangle in signs of the same triplicity and will thus emphasise the characteristics of the element involved.

Unaspected planets
Sometimes a planet (or, rarely, more than one) will make no aspect to any other planet in a chart. Depending on its sign and house position, this can indicate an area of the subject's life which is unsatisfactory.

CHAPTER 8
Assessing the Chart

The completed chart is made up of major and minor pieces of information, all of which have to be assessed individually and in relation to each other in order to obtain a balanced view of the chart as a whole. We will look at Jean's chart in this light.

The first thing to notice is that Virgo is on the Ascendant and the rulling planet is Mercury; the Midheaven is Gemini, also ruled by Mercury.

The Moon is the rising planet and the Sun occupies the 4th House in Capricorn. Uranus is in the 10th House, in Cancer, and is therefore the most elevated planet as it is the 'highest' planet in the chart.

Most of the planets are beneath the horizon, i.e. below the Ascendant/Descendant axis. The most emphasised quadrant is the second, whereas the third - Houses 7, 8 and 9 - is devoid of planetary occupation, although the Moon's north node is the 7th House, while the Part of Fortune is in the 9th.

There is an emphasis on Earth Signs; the quadruplicities are dominated by Cardinal signs; there are five angular planets (i.e. they occupy Angular houses) and no planet is unaspected. Houses 3, 7, 8, 9 and 11 are unoccupied, but no house is emphasised by three or more planets.

Looking at the major aspects, there are seven trines, five squares, three oppositions and two conjunctions. Finally, there are more planets in negative signs than in positive ones; only two are emphasised by exaltation, and none is in rulership, detriment or fall.

Before considering the significance of the individual planetary and sign positions, all these other factors must be weighed up carefully in order to get an idea of the chart as a whole and an indication of the type of personality of the subject.

So, reverting to the beginning, as Mercury rules both the 1st House and the MC, we would judge that the art of communication should be a dominating feature of Jean's personality. However, Mercury is retrograde in the 4th House, so there could be a stumbling block in the area associated with this house, her domestic environment: perhaps there is a feature of her home life that she dislikes, routine housework for instance.

The natural ruler of the 4th House is the Moon which, in Jean's chart, is the ruling planet, and the sign associated with the 4th House is Cancer, ruler of the 11th House cusp. Jean's Capricorn Sun in the 4th House suggests that she will be practical and hard-working, but only when it suits her. So, her home may seem comfortable and friendly to Jean's friends who will have to take her and her environment as they find them.

The Moon at the Ascendant identifies the subject closely with home and family life and, as it occupies Virgo, a regard for cleanliness, neatness and organisation is indicated. However, the Capricorn 4th House suggests that although Jean is an admirable planner she may not get around to implementing the plans on a regular basis.

Returning now to the chart ruler, Mercury, we have already noted that it also rules the MC and does so from the 4th House. Jean's MC suggests that she needs a career which will keep her intellectually and physically active because her mind and hands will always be restless and she will dislike boring, routine work.

Also, any job that Jean undertakes will have to help provide the home that she desires. So she may be prepared – up to a point – to take a job with which she is not entirely happy as long as it provides a sufficiently high renumeration to enable her to save for what she wants.

Jean is likely, in fact, to take the attitude that she can always swop her job but that her home is more permanent and she will not, therefore, be so prepared to make do here. This trait is verified by Uranus in the 10th House, signifying an unwillingness to conform to any set pattern. Further, it suggests that as long as Jean can regulate her life-style to suit herself and her own needs, she will be content.

Practical experience

It must be obvious by now that a picture has begun to emerge of various aspects of Jean's life and character just as a result of considering the chart ruler, rising planet and the focalising house of the chart, the 4th. This is, however, only a beginning of the long task that confronts an astrologer at this stage of an analysis and a beginner will need to gain experience before being able to interpret a chart fully.

Sometimes, too, a subject may refute totally part of your assessment or claim as the dominant factor some point that has merely been alluded to. This is not unusual and the student should not be unduly discouraged if it should occur. After all, none of us sees ourselves as others do – this consideration applies just as much to astrology as it does to any other field. Of course, it is also a fact of life that every astrologer will interpret a chart in a slightly different way.

It is rather like asking six photographers to photograph the same object with the same camera, then comparing the results. Each will produce a slightly different picture because each will have a slightly different approach. Similarly, if six astrologers analysed Jean's chart, their interpretations would vary slightly because each would exercise personal judgement when assessing the various factors involved.

So, the best advice that can be offered to any beginner is to experiment initially with the charts of those who are well-known to you. In this way you will more quickly realise which factors are most significant in an individual chart and which carry less weight. Only practical experience will promote ability so, the more charts you study, the more proficient you will become.

Further considerations

It should be remembered at this point that this book is designed to introduce the reader to astrology, which is why basic astronomy and astrological theory have not been included in its pages. Such information can prove very confusing to the beginner and is not strictly necessary in order to erect and interpret a natal chart. However, those sufficiently interested to want to take their studies further are advised to visit their local library or a reputable bookshop as there is plenty of reference material available for those who feel ready to cope with it.

Astrology is a vast subject and this book has only touched on one particular aspect of it – how to erect and interpret a natal chart. Even though this forms the basis of nearly all astrological work, it is only part of the picture and there will probably come the point when you ask yourself 'now what?'.

So, what is the next step? A few of you may rush off to join the nearest school of astrology or start delving into the intricacies of harmonics and such like. Most people, however, once they have mastered the art of reading a chart want to compare their own with those of people who are close to them or wish to know what possibilities the future has in store for them.

Both of these exercises are within the scope of those with some astrological experience and, although outside the intended range of this book, are worth explaining briefly so that the reader has some idea of what areas to explore next.

Synastry

Synastry is the term used for comparing two charts. It is possible, of course, to compare charts for a variety of reasons but, more often than not, a couple will want to know how well they are likely to get on together. But, whatever the reason, the method is the same and both charts will have to be studied carefully with particular reference to those planets and aspects that have a direct bearing on the relationship.

Sometimes, too, people will want to know whether or not a future event is likely to affect their relationship and, in such a case, the progressed charts of the people concerned will be studied and compared. For this to be carried out successfully, however, the birth data on which the charts are based must be accurate.

Progressions and transits

There are several different methods of progressing a chart but each relies on the natal data being absolutely correct because even a birth time that is a few minutes wrong can mean that the timing of future events will be wildly inaccurate. This is one reason why some astrologers prefer to look at transits for the date in question rather than calculate progressions. So, if there is any doubt that the birth data is accurate, do not bother with progressions as you would be wasting your time.

The difference between transits and progressions is straightforward. Progressions require additional mathematical calculations to be made which produce new configurations that are then inserted into the original birth chart or entered into a separate chart for comparison with the original. Transits are the study of the position of the planets for the day, or days, in question which are compared to their original positions in the natal chart.

Total accuracy is not needed when using transits because their effects are short-lived whereas, in certain circumstances, progressions may be effective for years. Oddly enough, progressional work is sometimes carried out in order to discover or verify a subject's birth time; this is known as rectification.

The process is relatively simple but can be very time-consuming, depending on how close the reported time of birth is to the actual. A series of charts is erected for times around the speculative birth time and these charts are then progressed until they 'fit in' or correspond to important events in the subject's life.

Conclusion

As may now be realised, astrology is a wide-ranging subject which offers may different areas for exploration and it is hoped, of course, that some at least will want to investigate this fascinating subject further.

Yet it is the birth chart – whether of a person, place or event – that is the starting point. Even those who have no desire to extend their studies can benefit from being able to erect and interpret a horoscope for it enables them to understand themselves and others better . . . and it can be fun finding out!

Appendix of Tables and Data

1 Planetary Dignities

Planet	Exalt	Fall	Ruler-ship	Detri-ment	Acci-dental Exalt	Acci-dental Fall	Acci-dental Dignity	Acci-dental Detriment
☉	♈	♎	♌	♒	1st	7th	5th	11th
☽	♉	♏	♋	♑	2nd	8th	4th	10th
☿	♒	♌	♊♍	♐♓	11th	5th	3rd-6th	9th-12th
♀	♓	♍	♉♎	♏♈	12th	6th	2nd-7th	8th-1st
♂	♑	♋	♈♏	♎♉	10th	4th	1st-8th	7th-2nd
♃	♋	♑	♐♓	♊♍	4th	10th	9th-12th	3rd-6th
♄	♎	♈	♑♒	♋♌	7th	1st	10th-11th	4th-5th
♅	♏	♉	♒	♌	8th	2nd	11th	5th
♆	♋	♑	♐♓	♊♍	4th	10th	9th-12th	3rd-6th
♇	♌	♒	♈♏	♎♉	5th	11th	1st-8th	7th-2nd

2 Conversion of Longitude to Time

DEGREES

°	h	m	°	h	m	°	h	m	°	h	m
0	0	00	30	2	00	60	4	00	90	6	00
1	0	04	31	2	04	61	4	04	91	6	04
2	0	08	32	2	08	62	4	08	92	6	08
3	0	12	33	2	12	63	4	12	93	6	12
4	0	16	34	2	16	64	4	16	94	6	16
5	0	20	35	2	20	65	4	20	95	6	20
6	0	24	36	2	24	66	4	24	96	6	24
7	0	28	37	2	28	67	4	28	97	6	28
8	0	32	38	2	32	68	4	32	98	6	32
9	0	36	39	2	36	69	4	36	99	6	36
10	0	40	40	2	40	70	4	40	100	6	40
11	0	44	41	2	44	71	4	44	101	6	44
12	0	48	42	2	48	72	4	48	102	6	48
13	0	52	43	2	52	73	4	52	103	6	52
14	0	56	44	2	56	74	4	56	104	6	56
15	1	00	45	3	00	75	5	00	105	7	00
16	1	04	46	3	04	76	5	04	106	7	04
17	1	08	47	3	08	77	5	08	107	7	08
18	1	12	48	3	12	78	5	12	108	7	12
19	1	16	49	3	16	79	5	16	109	7	16
20	1	20	50	3	20	80	5	20	110	7	20
21	1	24	51	3	24	81	5	24	111	7	24
22	1	28	52	3	28	82	5	28	112	7	28
23	1	32	53	3	32	83	5	32	113	7	32
24	1	36	54	3	36	84	5	36	114	7	36
25	1	40	55	3	40	85	5	40	115	7	40
26	1	44	56	3	44	86	5	44	116	7	44
27	1	48	57	3	48	87	5	48	117	7	48
28	1	52	58	3	52	88	5	52	118	7	52
29	1	56	59	3	56	89	5	56	119	7	56

°	h	m	°	h	m
120	8	00	150	10	00
121	8	04	151	10	04
122	8	08	152	10	08
123	8	12	153	10	12
124	8	16	154	10	16
125	8	20	155	10	20
126	8	24	156	10	24
127	8	28	157	10	28
128	8	32	158	10	32
129	8	36	159	10	36
130	8	40	160	10	40
131	8	44	161	10	44
132	8	48	162	10	48
133	8	52	163	10	52
134	8	56	164	10	56
135	9	00	165	11	00
136	9	04	166	11	04
137	9	08	167	11	08
138	9	12	168	11	12
139	9	16	169	11	16
140	9	20	170	11	20
141	9	24	171	11	24
142	9	28	172	11	28
143	9	32	173	11	32
144	9	36	174	11	36
145	9	40	175	11	40
146	9	44	176	11	44
147	9	48	177	11	48
148	9	52	178	11	52
149	9	56	179	11	56

3 Ephemeris for December 1950

NEW MOON—December 9, 9h. 28m. 25s. a.m.

24				DECEMBER, 1950					[R A P H A E L ' S	
D	Neptune.		Herschel.		Saturn.		Jupiter.		Mars.	
M	Lat.	Dec.	Lat.	Dec.	Lat.	Dec.	Lat.	Dec.	Lat.	Declin.
	° ′	° ′	° ′	° ′	° ′	° ′	° ′	° ′	° ′	° ′
1	1 N 35	5 S 54	0 N 19	23 N 29	2 N 8	1 N 37	1 S 8	12 S 33	1 S 18	23 S 21	23 S 14
3	1 36	5 56	0 19	23 30	2 8	1 34	1 8	12 28	1 17	23 7	23 0
5	1 36	5 57	0 19	23 30	2 9	1 31	1 7	12 22	1 17	22 52	22 44
7	1 36	5 58	0 19	23 30	2 9	1 29	1 7	12 16	1 17	22 36	22 28
9	1 36	5 59	0 19	23 31	2 10	1 26	1 7	12 10	1 16	22 19	22 10
11	1 36	6 0	0 19	23 31	2 10	1 24	1 7	12 4	1 16	22 1	21 51
13	1 36	6 0	0 19	23 31	2 11	1 22	1 6	11 57	1 15	21 42	21 32
15	1 36	6 1	0 19	23 32	2 11	1 20	1 6	11 50	1 15	21 22	21 11
17	1 36	6 2	0 19	23 32	2 12	1 18	1 6	11 43	1 14	21 1	20 50
19	1 36	6 3	0 19	23 32	2 12	1 17	1 6	11 36	1 14	20 38	20 27
21	1 36	6 3	0 20	23 33	2 13	1 15	1 5	11 29	1 13	20 16	20 4
23	1 37	6 4	0 20	23 33	2 13	1 14	1 5	11 21	1 13	19 52	19 40
25	1 37	6 5	0 20	23 33	2 14	1 13	1 5	11 14	1 12	19 27	19 15
27	1 37	6 5	0 20	23 34	2 15	1 12	1 5	11 6	1 12	19 1	18 49
29	1 37	6 6	0 20	23 34	2 15	1 11	1 4	10 58	1 11	18 36	18 22
31	1 37	6 6	0 20	23 34	2 16	1 11	1 4	10 49	1 10	18 8	

D	D	Sidereal	☉	☉	☽	☽	☽	MIDNIGHT	
M	W	Time.	Long.	Dec.	Long.	Lat.	Dec.	☽ Long.	☽ Dec.
		H. M. S.	° ′ ″	° ′	° ′ ″	° ′	° ′	° ′ ″	° ′
1	F	16 39 6	8♐43 33	21 S 46	24♌45 59	2 N 33	15 N 40	1♍ 7	24 13 N 0
2	S	16 43 3	9 44 23	21 55	7♍33 44	1 31	10 9	14 5 31	7 9
3	☉	16 46 59	10 45 14	22 4	20 43 15	0 23	4 2	27 27 23	0 49
4	M	16 50 56	11 46 7	22 12	4♎18 15	0 S 49	2 S 27	11♎16 8	5 S 46
5	Tu	16 54 52	12 47 2	22 20	18 21 7	2 0	9 3	25 33	8 12 16
6	W	16 58 49	13 47 57	22 28	2♏51 53	3 6	15 22	10♏16 52	18 18
7	Th	17 2 45	14 48 54	22 35	17 47 20	4 0	20 59	25 22 18	23 21
8	F	17 6 42	15 49 52	22 42	3♐ 0 33	4 39	25 20	10♐40 44	26 52
9	S	17 10 38	16 50 50	22 48	18 21 22	4 58	27 53	26 0 57	28 23
10	☉	17 14 35	17 51 50	22 54	3♑58 0	4 56	28 20	11♑11 8	27 47
11	M	17 18 32	18 52 51	22 59	18 39 9	4 33	26 40	26 1 4	25 8
12	Tu	17 22 28	19 53 52	23 4	3♒16 7	3 53	23 12	10♒23 48	20 58
13	W	17 26 25	20 54 54	23 8	17 23 52	2 59	18 28	24 16 16	15 47
14	Th	17 30 21	21 55 56	23 12	1♓ 1 9	1 57	12 56	7♓38 50	10 0
15	F	17 34 18	22 56 59	23 16	14 44 0	0 51	7 1	20 34 23	4 0
16	S	17 38 14	23 58 3	23 19	26 53 22	0 N 16	0 59	3♈ 7 21	2 N 0
17	☉	17 42 11	24 59 6	23 21	9♈16 56	1 21	4 N 55	15 22 47	7 49
18	M	17 46 7	26 0 10	23 23	21 25 32	2 20	10 32	27 25 47	13 10
19	Tu	17 50 4	27 1 15	23 25	3♉24 5	3 13	15 40	9♉20 58	18 8
20	W	17 54 1	28 2 19	23 26	15 16 55	3 56	20 11	21 12 20	22 9
21	Th	17 57 57	29 3 24	23 27	27 7 37	4 29	23 53	3♊ 3 4	25 22
22	F	18 1 54	0♑ 4 30	23 27	8♊11 58	4 50	26 35	14 55 34	27 30
23	S	18 5 50	1 5 36	23 27	20 53 2	4 59	28 20	8♋52 12	27 23
24	☉	18 9 47	2 6 42	23 26	2♋51 13	4 55	28 20	8 52 12	27 56
25	M	18 13 43	3 7 48	23 25	14 54 36	4 37	27 12	20 58 32	26 9
26	Tu	18 17 40	4 8 55	23 23	27 4 8	4 7	24 47	3♌11 34	23 8
27	W	18 21 36	5 10 3	23 21	9♌21 1	3 24	21 12	15 32 40	19 2
28	Th	18 25 33	6 11 10	23 18	21 46 48	2 32	16 39	28 3 14	14 4
29	F	18 29 30	7 12 18	23 15	4♍23 42	1 31	11 19	10♍47 9	8 26
30	S	18 33 26	8 13 27	23 12	17 14 26	0 25	5 25	23 45 59	2 19
31	☉	18 37 23	9 14 36	23 8	0♎22 11	0 S 45	0 S 50	7♎ 3 25	4 S 1

FIRST QUARTER—December 16, 5h. 56m. 21s. a.m.

© W. Foulsham & Co. Ltd. Reproduced from *Raphael's Ephemeris* with permission of the publishers W. Foulsham & Co. Ltd.

121

FULL MOON—December 24, 10*h*. 22*m*. 46*s*. *a.m.*

EPHEMERIS] **DECEMBER 1950** 25

D M	Venus. Lat. ° ′	Venus. Declin. ° ′	Venus. Declin. ° ′	Mercury. Lat. ° ′	Mercury. Declin. ° ′	Mercury. Declin. ° ′	☽ Node. ° ′
1	0 S 4	22 S 26	22 S 38	2 S 18	25 S 38	25 S 43	24 ♓ 24
3	0 9	22 49	22 59	2 21	25 46	25 48	24 18
5	0 14	23 8	23 17	2 22	25 49	25 48	24 11
7	0 18	23 25	23 32	2 21	25 45	25 41	24 5
9	0 23	23 39	23 45	2 18	25 36	25 30	23 59
11	0 28	23 50	23 55	2 12	25 21	25 12	23 52
13	0 32	23 58	24 1	2 3	25 1	24 50	23 46
15	0 37	24 4	24 5	1 51	24 37	24 23	23 39
17	0 41	24 6	24 6	1 34	24 8	23 52	23 33
19	0 45	24 5	24 4	1 13	23 36	23 19	23 27
21	0 50	24 1	23 58	0 46	23 2	22 45	23 20
23	0 54	23 55	23 50	0 15	22 28	22 11	23 14
25	0 58	23 45	23 39	0 N 20	21 55	21 40	23 8
27	1 2	23 32	23 25	0 59	21 26	21 12	23 1
29	1 5	23 17	23 8	1 38	21 0	20 48	22 55
31	1 8	22 58		2 14	20 38		22 49

Mutual Aspects.

1. ☉⊽♅. ♀⊥♂, Q♄.
2. ♂⊽♇.
4. ♀P♂, P♇. ♂P♇.
5. ☉Q♄. ☿✱♃, □♄, Q♆.
6. ♀✱♆, △♇. [♀Q♃.
7. ☉P♂.
8. ☿⚼♇. ♀P♅. ♂⊥♃.
11. ☉Q♃, ✱♆, P♇. ☿☍♅.
12. ☉△♇. 14. ♀⊻♂
15. ♀Q♆. ☿±♇.
16. ♀✱♃, □♄.
17. ☿P♀. ♂△♄.
18. ♀⚼♇. ♂⊻♃. 19. ☿P♅.
20. ☉P☿, ⊥♂.
21. ☿∠♃, P♇. ♀☍♅.
23. ☉Q♆, ☿∠♃.
24. ☉□♄.
25. ☉✱♃. ♀±♇. ♂⊽♅.
26. ☉⚼♇.
27. ☿☌♀. ♀P♅.
29. ☉P♀, ☍♅.
30. ♀∠♃, □♆, ⊽ & P♇.
31. ☉P♇. ☿⊻♂. [♃⚼♆.

D M	♆ Long. ° ′	♅ Long. ° ′	♄ Long. ° ′	♃ Long. ° ′	♂ Long. ° ′	♀ Long. ° ′	☿ Long. ° ′	☉	♇	♆	♅	♄	♃	♂	♀	☿
1	18 ♎ 50	8 ♋ 36	0 ♎ 51	29 ♒ 58	19 ♑ 14	13 ♐ 3	24 ♐ 49		☌	✱	∠	⊻	☍			△
2	18 52	8 ℞ 33	0 55	0 ♓ 5	20 0	14 18	26 17	□		∠	✱			⚼		
𝔖	18 53	8 31	0 59	0 12	20 46	15 34	27 44		⊻	⊻				△	□	
4	18 55	8 29	1 3	0 20	21 33	16 49	29 11		∠		□	☌				□
5	18 56	8 27	1 7	0 28	22 19	18 4	0 ♑ 36	✱	✱	☌			⚼	□	✱	
6	18 58	8 24	1 11	0 36	23 6	19 20	2 1	∠			△	⊻	△		∠	✱
7	18 59	8 22	1 15	0 44	23 52	20 35	3 25	⊻	□	⊻	⚼	∠		✱	⊻	∠
8	19 0	8 20	1 18	0 52	24 39	21 51	4 47			∠		✱	□	∠		⊻
9	19 2	8 17	1 22	1 0	25 26	23 6	6 8	☌	△	✱				⊻	☌	
𝔖	19 3	8 15	1 25	1 9	26 13	24 22	7 27		⚼		☍	□	✱			☌
11	19 4	8 13	1 28	1 17	26 59	25 37	8 43	⊻		□			∠			
12	19 6	8 10	1 32	1 26	27 46	26 52	9 58	∠				△	⊻	☌	⊻	
13	19 7	8 8	1 35	1 35	28 33	28 8	11 9	✱	☍	△	⚼	⚼			∠	⊻
14	19 8	8 5	1 38	1 44	29 20	29 23	12 17			⚼			☌	⊻	✱	∠
15	19 10	8 3	1 41	1 53	0 ♒ 6	0 ♑ 39	13 21				△			∠		✱
16	19 11	8 0	1 44	2 2	0 53	1 54	14 21	□				☍	⊻	✱	□	
𝔖	19 12	7 58	1 46	2 12	1 40	3 10	15 16		⚼		□					
18	19 13	7 56	1 49	2 21	2 27	4 25	16 4	△	△	☍			∠			□
19	19 14	7 53	1 52	2 31	3 14	5 40	16 46				✱		✱	□	△	
20	19 15	7 50	1 54	2 41	4 1	6 56	17 21	⚼	□			⚼				△
21	19 16	7 48	1 57	2 51	4 48	8 11	17 47				∠	△	□		⚼	⚼
22	19 17	7 45	1 59	3 1	5 35	9 26	18 4			⚼	⊻			△		
23	19 18	7 43	2 1	3 11	6 22	10 42	18 ℞ 10		✱	△				⚼		
𝔖	19 19	7 40	2 3	3 21	7 9	11 57	18 6	☍	∠		☌	□	△			
25	19 20	7 38	2 5	3 32	7 56	13 13	17 50		⊻	□			⚼		☍	☍
26	19 21	7 35	2 7	3 42	8 43	14 28	17 23					✱				
27	19 22	7 32	2 9	3 53	9 30	15 43	16 43				⊻			☍		
28	19 23	7 30	2 10	4 3	10 18	16 59	15 53	⚼	☌	✱	∠	∠				
29	19 24	7 27	2 12	4 14	11 5	18 14	14 52	△		∠	✱	⊻	☍		⚼	⚼
30	19 24	7 25	2 13	4 25	11 52	19 29	13 43		⊻	⊻					△	△
𝔖	19 25	7 22	2 15	4 36	12 39	20 45	12 27		∠			☌				

LAST QUARTER—December 2, 4*h*. 21*m*. 38*s*. *p.m.*

© W. Foulsham & Co. Ltd. Reproduced from *Raphael's Ephemeris* with permission of the publishers W. Foulsham & Co. Ltd.

4 Tables of Houses for London

TABLES OF HOUSES FOR LONDON, Latitude 51° 32′ *N.*

Sidereal Time. H.	M.	S.	10 ♈ °	11 ♉ °	12 ♊ °	Ascen ♋ °	′	2 ♌ °	3 ♍ °
0	0	0	0	9	22	26	36	12	3
0	3	40	1	10	23	27	17	13	3
0	7	20	2	11	24	27	56	14	4
0	11	0	3	12	25	28	42	15	5
0	14	41	4	13	25	29	17	15	6
0	18	21	5	14	26	29	55	16	7
0	22	2	6	15	27	0 ♌	34	17	8
0	25	42	7	16	28	1	14	18	8
0	29	23	8	17	29	1	55	18	9
0	33	4	9	18	♋	2	33	19	10
0	36	45	10	19	1	3	14	20	11
0	40	26	11	20	1	3	54	20	12
0	44	8	12	21	2	4	33	21	13
0	47	50	13	22	3	5	12	22	14
0	51	32	14	23	4	5	52	23	15
0	55	14	15	24	5	6	30	23	15
0	58	57	16	25	6	7	9	24	16
1	2	40	17	26	6	7	50	25	17
1	6	23	18	27	7	8	30	26	18
1	10	7	19	28	8	9	9	26	19
1	13	51	20	29	9	9	48	27	19
1	17	35	21	♊	10	10	28	28	20
1	21	20	22	1	10	11	8	28	21
1	25	6	23	2	11	11	48	29	22
1	28	52	24	3	12	12	28	♍	23
1	32	38	25	4	13	13	8	1	24
1	36	25	26	5	14	13	48	1	25
1	40	12	27	6	14	14	28	2	25
1	44	0	28	7	15	15	8	3	26
1	47	48	29	8	16	15	48	4	27
1	51	37	30	9	17	16	28	4	28

Sidereal Time. H.	M.	S.	10 ♉ °	11 ♊ °	12 ♋ °	Ascen ♌ °	′	2 ♍ °	3 ♍ °
1	51	37	0	9	17	16	28	4	28
1	55	27	1	10	18	17	8	5	29
1	59	17	2	11	19	17	48	6	♎
2	3	8	3	12	19	18	28	7	1
2	6	59	4	13	20	19	9	8	2
2	10	51	5	14	21	19	49	9	2
2	14	44	6	15	22	20	29	9	3
2	18	37	7	16	22	21	10	10	4
2	22	31	8	17	23	21	51	11	5
2	26	25	9	18	24	22	32	11	6
2	30	20	10	19	25	23	14	12	7
2	34	16	11	20	25	23	55	13	8
2	38	13	12	21	26	24	36	14	9
2	42	10	13	22	27	25	17	15	10
2	46	8	14	23	28	25	58	15	11
2	50	7	15	24	29	26	40	16	12
2	54	7	16	25	29	27	22	17	12
2	58	7	17	26	♌	28	4	18	13
3	2	8	18	27	1	28	46	18	14
3	6	9	19	27	2	29	28	19	15
3	10	12	20	28	3	0 ♍	12	20	16
3	14	15	21	29	3	0	54	21	17
3	18	19	22	♋	4	1	36	22	18
3	22	23	23	1	5	2	20	22	19
3	26	29	24	2	6	3	2	23	20
3	30	35	25	3	7	3	45	24	21
3	34	41	26	4	7	4	28	25	22
3	38	49	27	5	8	5	11	26	23
3	42	57	28	6	9	5	54	27	24
3	47	6	29	7	10	6	38	27	25
3	51	15	30	8	11	7	21	28	25

Sidereal Time. H.	M.	S.	10 ♊ °	11 ♋ °	12 ♌ °	Ascen ♍ °	′	2 ♍ °	3 ♎ °
3	51	15	0	8	11	7	21	28	25
3	55	25	1	9	12	8	5	29	26
3	59	36	2	10	12	8	49	♎	27
4	3	48	3	10	13	9	33	1	28
4	8	0	4	11	14	10	17	2	29
4	12	13	5	12	15	11	2	2	♏
4	16	26	6	13	16	11	46	3	1
4	20	40	7	14	17	12	30	4	2
4	24	55	8	15	17	13	15	5	3
4	29	10	9	16	18	14	0	6	4
4	33	26	10	17	19	14	45	7	5
4	37	42	11	18	20	15	30	8	6
4	41	59	12	19	21	16	15	8	7
4	46	16	13	20	21	17	0	9	8
4	50	34	14	21	22	17	45	10	9
4	54	52	15	22	23	18	30	11	10
4	59	10	16	23	24	19	16	12	11
5	3	29	17	24	25	20	3	13	12
5	7	49	18	25	26	20	49	14	13
5	12	9	19	25	27	21	35	14	14
5	16	29	20	26	28	22	20	15	14
5	20	49	21	27	28	23	6	16	15
5	25	9	22	28	29	23	51	17	16
5	29	30	23	29	♍	24	37	18	17
5	33	51	24	♌	1	25	23	19	18
5	38	12	25	1	2	26	9	20	19
5	42	34	26	2	3	26	55	21	20
5	46	55	27	3	4	27	41	21	21
5	51	17	28	4	4	28	27	22	22
5	55	38	29	5	5	29	13	23	23
6	0	0	30	6	6	30	0	24	24

Sidereal Time. H.	M.	S.	10 ♋ °	11 ♌ °	12 ♍ °	Ascen ♎ °	′	2 ♎ °	3 ♏ °
6	0	0	0	6	6	0	0	24	24
6	4	22	1	7	7	0	47	25	25
6	8	43	2	8	8	1	33	26	26
6	13	5	3	9	9	2	19	27	27
6	17	26	4	10	10	3	5	27	28
6	21	48	5	11	10	3	51	28	29
6	26	9	6	12	11	4	37	29	♐
6	30	30	7	13	12	5	23	♏	1
6	34	51	8	14	13	6	9	1	2
6	39	11	9	15	14	6	55	2	3
6	43	31	10	16	15	7	40	2	4
6	47	51	11	16	16	8	26	3	4
6	52	11	12	17	16	9	12	4	5
6	56	31	13	18	17	9	58	5	6
7	0	50	14	19	18	10	43	6	7
7	5	8	15	20	19	11	28	7	8
7	9	26	16	21	20	12	14	8	9
7	13	44	17	22	21	12	59	8	10
7	18	1	18	23	22	13	45	9	11
7	22	18	19	24	23	14	30	10	12
7	26	34	20	25	24	15	15	11	13
7	30	50	21	26	25	16	0	12	14
7	35	5	22	27	25	16	45	13	15
7	39	20	23	28	26	17	30	13	16
7	43	34	24	29	27	18	15	14	17
7	47	47	25	♍	28	18	59	15	18
7	52	0	26	1	29	19	43	16	19
7	56	12	27	2	29	20	27	17	20
8	0	24	28	3	♎	21	11	18	20
8	4	35	29	4	1	21	56	18	21
8	8	45	30	5	2	22	40	19	22

Sidereal Time. H.	M.	S.	10 ♌ °	11 ♍ °	12 ♎ °	Ascen ♎ °	′	2 ♏ °	3 ♐ °
8	8	45	0	5	2	22	40	19	22
8	12	54	1	5	3	23	24	20	23
8	17	3	2	6	3	24	7	21	24
8	21	11	3	7	4	24	50	22	25
8	25	19	4	8	5	25	34	23	26
8	29	26	5	9	6	26	18	23	27
8	33	31	6	10	7	27	1	24	28
8	37	37	7	11	8	27	44	25	29
8	41	41	8	12	8	28	26	26	♑
8	45	45	9	13	9	29	8	27	1
8	49	48	10	14	10	29	50	27	2
8	53	51	11	15	11	0 ♏	32	28	3
8	57	52	12	16	12	1	15	29	4
9	1	53	13	17	12	1	58	♐	4
9	5	53	14	18	13	2	39	1	5
9	9	53	15	18	14	3	21	1	6
9	13	52	16	19	15	4	3	2	7
9	17	50	17	20	16	4	44	3	8
9	21	47	18	21	16	5	26	3	9
9	25	44	19	22	17	6	7	4	10
9	29	40	20	23	18	6	48	5	11
9	33	35	21	24	18	7	29	5	12
9	37	29	22	25	19	8	9	6	13
9	41	23	23	26	20	8	50	7	14
9	45	16	24	27	21	9	31	8	15
9	49	9	25	28	22	10	11	9	16
9	53	1	26	28	23	10	51	9	17
9	56	52	27	29	23	11	32	10	18
10	0	43	28	♎	24	12	12	11	19
10	4	33	29	1	25	12	53	12	20
10	8	23	30	2	26	13	33	13	20

Sidereal Time. H.	M.	S.	10 ♍ °	11 ♎ °	12 ♎ °	Ascen ♏ °	′	2 ♐ °	3 ♑ °
10	8	23	0	2	26	13	33	13	20
10	12	12	1	3	26	14	13	14	21
10	16	0	2	4	27	14	53	15	22
10	19	48	3	5	28	15	33	15	23
10	23	35	4	5	29	16	13	16	24
10	27	22	5	6	29	16	52	17	25
10	31	8	6	7	♏	17	32	18	26
10	34	54	7	8	1	18	12	19	27
10	38	40	8	9	2	18	52	20	28
10	42	25	9	10	2	19	31	20	29
10	46	9	10	11	3	20	11	21	♒
10	49	53	11	11	4	20	50	22	1
10	53	37	12	12	4	21	30	23	2
10	57	20	13	13	5	22	9	24	3
11	1	3	14	14	6	22	49	24	4
11	4	46	15	15	7	23	28	25	5
11	8	28	16	16	7	24	8	26	6
11	12	10	17	17	8	24	47	27	8
11	15	52	18	17	9	25	27	28	9
11	19	34	19	18	10	26	6	29	10
11	23	15	20	19	10	26	45	♑	11
11	26	56	21	20	11	27	25	0	12
11	30	37	22	21	12	28	5	1	13
11	34	18	23	22	13	28	44	2	14
11	37	58	24	23	13	29	24	3	15
11	41	39	25	23	14	0 ♐	3	4	16
11	45	19	26	24	15	0	43	5	17
11	49	0	27	25	15	1	23	6	18
11	52	40	28	26	16	2	3	6	19
11	56	20	29	27	17	2	43	7	20
12	0	0	30	27	17	3	23	8	21

© W. Foulsham & Co. Ltd. Reproduced from *Raphael's Ephemeris* with permission of the publishers W. Foulsham & Co. Ltd.

4 Tables of Houses for London (cont.)

TABLES OF HOUSES FOR LONDON, Latitude 51° 32′ N.

Sidereal Time	10	11	12	Ascen	2	3	Sidereal Time	10	11	12	Ascen	2	3	Sidereal Time	10	11	12	Ascen	2	3
	♎	♎	♏	♐	♑	♒		♏	♏	♐	♐	♒	♓		♐	♐	♑	♒	♓	♈
H. M. S.	°	°	°	° ′	°	°	H. M. S.	°	°	°	° ′	°	°	H. M. S.	°	°	°	° ′	°	°
12 0 0	0	27	17	3 23	8	21	13 51 37	0	22	10	25	20	10	27 15 51 15	0	18	6	27	15	26 6
12 3 40	1	28	18	4 4	9	23	13 55 27	1	23	11	26	10	11	28 15 55 25	1	19	7	28	42	28 7
12 7 20	2	29	19	4 45	10	24	13 59 17	2	24	11	27	2	12	♈ 15 59 36	2	20	8	0♒	11	♈ 9
12 11 0	3	♏	20	5 26	11	25	14 3 8	3	25	12	27	53	14	1 16 3 48	3	21	9	1	42	2 10
12 14 41	4	1	20	6 7	12	26	14 6 59	4	26	13	28	45	15	2 16 8 0	4	22	10	3	16	3 11
12 18 21	5	1	21	6 48	13	27	14 10 51	5	26	14	29	36	16	4 16 12 13	5	23	11	4	53	5 12
12 22 2	6	2	22	7 29	14	28	14 14 44	6	27	15	0♑	29	18	5 16 16 26	6	24	12	6	32	7 14
12 25 42	7	3	23	8 10	15	29	14 18 37	7	28	15	1	23	19	6 16 20 40	7	25	13	8	13	9 15
12 29 23	8	4	23	8 51	16	♓	14 22 31	8	29	16	2	18	20	8 16 24 55	8	26	14	9	57	11 16
12 33 4	9	5	24	9 33	17	2	14 26 25	9	♐	17	3	14	22	9 16 29 10	9	27	16	11	44	12 17
12 36 45	10	6	25	10 15	18	3	14 30 20	10	1	18	4	11	23	10 16 33 26	10	28	17	13	34	14 18
12 40 26	11	6	25	10 57	19	4	14 34 16	11	2	19	5	9	25	11 16 37 42	11	29	18	15	26	16 20
12 44 8	12	7	26	11 40	20	5	14 38 13	12	2	20	6	7	26	13 16 41 59	12	♑	19	17	20	18 21
12 47 50	13	8	27	12 22	21	6	14 42 10	13	3	20	7	6	28	14 16 46 16	13	1	20	19	18	20 22
12 51 32	14	9	28	13 4	22	7	14 46 8	14	4	21	8	6	29	15 16 50 34	14	2	21	21	22	21 23
12 55 14	15	10	28	13 47	23	9	14 50 7	15	5	22	9	8	♓	17 16 54 52	15	3	22	23	29	23 25
12 58 57	16	11	29	14 30	24	10	14 54 7	16	6	23	10	11	2	18 16 59 10	16	4	24	25	36	25 26
13 2 40	17	11	♐	15 14	25	11	14 58 7	17	7	24	11	15	4	19 17 3 29	17	5	25	27	4♈	27 27
13 6 23	18	12	1	15 59	26	12	15 2 8	18	8	25	12	20	6	21 17 7 49	18	6	26	0♈	0	28 28
13 10 7	19	13	1	16 44	27	13	15 6 9	19	9	26	13	27	8	22 17 12 19	19	7	27	2	19	♉ 29
13 13 51	20	14	2	17 29	28	15	15 10 12	20	9	27	14	35	9	23 17 16 29	20	8	29	4	40	2 ♊
13 17 35	21	15	3	18 14	29	16	15 14 15	21	10	27	15	43	11	24 17 20 49	21	♒	7	2	3	1
13 21 20	22	16	4	19 0♒	17	15 18 19	22	11	28	16	52	13	2	17 25 9	22	10	1	9	26	5 2
13 25 6	23	16	4	19 45	1	18	15 22 23	23	12	29	18	3	14	27 17 29 30	23	11	3	11	54	7 3
13 28 52	24	17	5	20 31	2	20	15 26 29	24	13	♏	19	16	16	28 17 33 51	24	12	4	14	24	8 5
13 32 38	25	18	6	21 18	4	21	15 30 35	25	14	1	20	32	17	29 17 38 12	25	13	5	16	58	10 6
13 36 25	26	19	7	22 6	5	22	15 34 41	26	15	2	21	48	19	♉ 17 42 34	26	14	7	19	31	11 7
13 40 12	27	20	7	22 54	6	23	15 38 49	27	16	3	23	8	21	2 17 46 55	27	15	8	22	5	13 8
13 44 0	28	21	8	23 42	7	25	15 42 57	28	17	4	24	29	22	3 17 51 17	28	16	10	24	41	14 9
13 47 48	29	21	9	24 31	8	26	15 47 6	29	18	5	25	51	24	5 17 55 38	29	17	11	27	21	16 10
13 51 37	30	22	10	25 20	10	27	15 51 15	30	18	6	27	15	26	6 18 0 0	30	18	13	30	0	17 11

Sidereal Time	10	11	12	Ascen	2	3	Sidereal Time	10	11	12	Ascen	2	3	Sidereal Time	10	11	12	Ascen	2	3
	♑	♒	♒	♈	♉	♊		♒	♒	♈	♊	♊	♋		♓	♈	♉	♋	♋	♌
H. M. S.	°	°	°	° ′	°	°	H. M. S.	°	°	°	° ′	°	°	H. M. S.	°	°	°	° ′	°	°
18 0 0	0	18	13	0 0	17	11	20 8 45	0	24	4	2 45	24	12	22 8 23	0	3	20	4 38	20	8
18 4 22	1	20	14	2 39	19	13	20 12 54	1	25	6	4 9	25	12	22 12 12	1	4	21	5 28	21	8
18 8 43	2	21	16	5 19	20	14	20 17 3	2	27	7	5 32	26	13	22 16 0	2	6	23	6 17	22	9
18 13 5	3	22	17	7 55	22	15	20 21 11	3	28	9	6 53	27	14	22 19 48	3	7	24	7 5	23	10
18 17 26	4	23	19	10 29	23	16	20 25 19	4	29	11	8 14	28	15	22 23 35	4	8	25	7 53	23	11
18 21 48	5	24	20	13 2	25	17	20 29 26	5	♈	13	9 27	29	16	22 27 22	5	9	26	8 42	24	12
18 26 9	6	25	22	15 36	26	18	20 33 31	6	2	14	10 44	♋	17	22 31 8	6	10	28	9 29	25	13
18 30 30	7	26	23	18 6	28	19	20 37 37	7	3	16	11 58	1	18	22 34 54	7	12	29	10 16	26	14
18 34 51	8	27	25	20 20	29	20	20 41 41	8	4	18	13 9	2	19	22 38 40	8	13	♊	11 2	26	14
18 39 11	9	29	27	22 59	♊	21	20 45 45	9	6	19	14 18	3	20	22 42 25	9	14	1	11 47	27	15
18 43 31	10	♒	28	25 22	1	22	20 49 48	10	7	21	15 25	3	21	22 46 9	10	15	2	12 31	28	16
18 47 51	11	1	♓	27 42	2	23	20 53 51	11	8	23	16 31	4	22	22 49 53	11	17	3	13 16	29	17
18 52 11	12	2	2	29 58	4	24	20 57 52	12	9	24	17 39	5	22	22 53 37	12	18	4	14	♌	19
18 56 31	13	3	3	2 ♉ 13	5	25	21 1 53	13	11	26	18 44	6	23	22 57 20	13	19	5	14 45	♌	19
19 0 50	14	4	5	4 24	6	26	21 5 53	14	12	28	19 48	7	24	23 1 3	14	20	6	15 28	1	19
19 5 8	15	6	7	6 30	8	27	21 9 53	15	13	29	20 51	8	25	23 4 46	15	21	7	16 11	1	20
19 9 26	16	7	9	8 36	9	28	21 13 51	15	8	21	53	9	26	23 8 28	16	23	8	16 54	2	21
19 13 44	17	8	10	10 40	10	29	21 17 50	17	16	2	22 55	10	27	23 12 10	17	24	9	17 37	3	22
19 18 1	18	9	12	12 39	11	♋	21 21 47	18	17	4	23 57	11	28	23 15 52	18	25	10	18 20	4	23
19 22 18	19	10	14	14 35	12	1	21 25 44	19	19	5	24 58	12	29	23 19 34	19	26	11	19 3	5	24
19 26 34	20	12	16	16 28	13	2	21 29 40	20	20	7	25 58	12	29	23 23 15	20	27	12	19 45	5	24
19 30 50	21	13	18	18 17	14	3	21 33 31	21	22	8	26 44	13	♌	23 26 56	21	29	13	20 26	6	25
19 35 5	22	14	19	20 3	16	4	21 37 29	22	23	10	27 40	14	1	23 30 37	22	♉	14	21 8	7	26
19 39 20	23	15	21	21 48	17	5	21 41 23	23	24	11	28 34	15	2	23 34 18	23	1	15	21 50	8	27
19 43 34	24	16	23	23 29	18	6	21 45 16	24	25	13	29 30	15	3	23 37 58	24	2	16	22 31	9	28
19 47 47	25	18	25	25 9	19	7	21 49 9	25	26	14	0♋ 22	16	4	23 41 39	25	3	17	23 12	9	28
19 52 0	26	19	27	26 45	20	8	21 53 1	15	17	4	23 45	19	26	4	18 23	53	9	29		
19 56 12	27	20	28	28 18	21	9	21 56 52	27	29	16	2 7	18	5	23 49 0	27	5	19	24 32	10	♍
20 0 24	28	21	♈	29 49	22	10	22 0 43	28	♉	17	2 55	19	6	23 52 40	28	6	20	25 15	11	1
20 4 35	29	23	2	1 ♊19	23	11	22 4 33	29	2	19	3 48	19	7	23 56 20	29	8	21	25 56	12	2
20 8 45	30	24	4	2 45	24	12	22 8 23	30	3	20	4 38	20	8	24 0 0	30	9	22	26 36	13	3

© W. Foulsham & Co. Ltd. Reproduced from *Raphael's Ephemeris* with permission of the publishers W. Foulsham & Co. Ltd.

5 House Classification

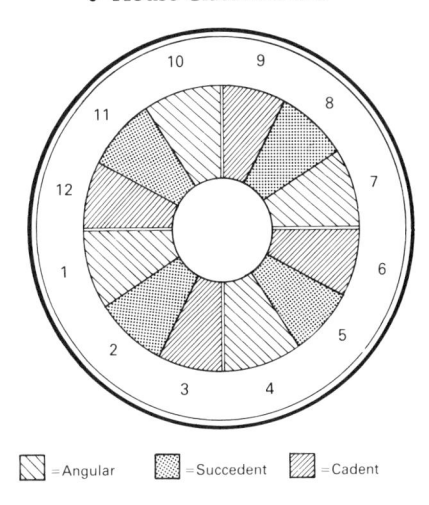

= Angular   = Succedent   = Cadent

6 British Summer Time

Note: The change from GMT to BST (GMT + 1 hour) and the reversion occurs at 2 a.m. on the dates given except where marked†.

For a trial period of two years, 1981 and 1982, BST was in force from 1 a.m. on the dates given and reverted at 1 a.m.

Year	Duration	Year	Duration
1916	May 21st – October 1st	1930	April 13th – October 5th
1917	April 8th – September 17th	1931	April 19th – October 4th
1918	March 24th – September 30th	1932	April 17th – October 2nd
1919	March 30th – September 29th	1933	April 9th – October 8th
1920	March 28th – October 25th	1934	April 22nd – October 7th
1921	April 3rd – October 3rd	1935	April 14th – October 6th
1922	March 26th – October 8th	1936	April 19th – October 4th
1923	April 22nd – September 16th	1937	April 18th – October 3rd
1924	April 13th – September 21st	1938	April 10th – October 2nd
1925	April 19th – October 4th	1939	April 16th – November 19th
1926	April 18th – October 3rd	1940	February 25th – (continues)
1927	April 10th – October 2nd	*1941	All year
1928	April 22nd – October 7th	*1942	All year
1929	April 21st – October 6th	*1943	All year

*1944 All year
*1945 January 1st – October 7th
1946 April 14th – October 6th
*1947 March 16th – November 2nd
1948 March 14th – October 31st
1949 April 3rd – October 30th
1950 April 16th – October 22nd
1951 April 15th – October 21st
1952 April 20th – October 26th
1953 April 19th – October 4th
1954 April 11th – October 3rd
1955 April 17th – October 2nd
1956 April 22nd – October 7th
1957 April 14th – October 6th
1958 April 20th – October 5th
1959 April 19th – October 4th
1960 April 10th – October 2nd
1961 March 26th – October 29th
1962 March 25th – October 28th
1963 March 31st – October 27th
1964 March 22nd – October 25th

1965 March 21st – October 24th
1966 March 20th – October 23rd
1967 March 19th – October 29th
1968 February 18th – (continues)
1969 All year
1970 All year
1971 – October 31st (ended)
1972 March 19th – October 29th
1973 March 18th – October 28th
1974 March 17th – October 27th
1975 March 16th – October 26th
1976 March 21st – October 24th
1977 March 20th – October 23rd
1978 March 19th – October 29th
1979 March 18th – October 28th
1980 March 16th – October 26th
1981 March 29th – October 25th†
1982 March 28th – October 24th†
1983 March 27th – October 23rd
1984 March 18th – October 28th
1985 March 17th – October 27th

*This indicates years when Double Summer Time/Daylight Saving Time (GMT plus 2 hours) was in force and special care should be taken when erecting a chart for anyone born within this period.

As with BST, the change from BST to DST and the reversion occur at 2 a.m. on the dates given in the following table.

British Standard Time, also equal to GMT + 1 hour, was the name given to the time system in use between February 18, 1968 and October 31, 1971. As the effects were the same as British Summer Time, the same abbreviation (BST) has been used.

Double Summer Time/Daylight Saving Time (UK)

Year Duration of DST
(GMT + 2 hours)

1941 May 4th – August 10th
1942 April 5th – August 9th
1943 April 4th – August 15th
1944 April 2nd – September 17th

Year Duration of DST
(GMT + 2 hours)

1945 April 2nd – July 15th
1946 Not observed
1947 April 13th – August 10th

Footnote: Reproduced with permission from data supplied by the Science Research Council.

7 Sidereal Time Correction

MIN	0h m s	1h m s	2h m s	3h m s	4h m s	5h m s	6h m s	7h m s	8h m s	9h m s	10h m s	11h m s	MIN
0	0 0	0 10	0 20	0 30	0 39	0 49	0 59	1 9	1 19	1 29	1 39	1 48	0
1	0 0	0 10	0 20	0 30	0 40	0 49	0 59	1 9	1 19	1 29	1 39	1 49	1
2	0 0	0 10	0 20	0 30	0 40	0 50	0 59	1 9	1 19	1 29	1 39	1 49	2
3	0 0	0 10	0 20	0 30	0 40	0 50	0 60	1 9	1 19	1 29	1 39	1 49	3
4	0 1	0 11	0 20	0 30	0 40	0 50	0 60	1 10	1 20	1 29	1 39	1 49	4
5	0 1	0 11	0 21	0 30	0 40	0 50	0 60	1 10	1 20	1 30	1 39	1 49	5
6	0 1	0 11	0 21	0 31	0 40	0 50	1 0	1 10	1 20	1 30	1 40	1 49	6
7	0 1	0 11	0 21	0 31	0 41	0 50	1 0	1 10	1 20	1 30	1 40	1 50	7
8	0 1	0 11	0 21	0 31	0 41	0 51	1 0	1 10	1 20	1 30	1 40	1 50	8
9	0 1	0 11	0 21	0 31	0 41	0 51	1 1	1 10	1 20	1 30	1 40	1 50	9
10	0 2	0 11	0 21	0 31	0 41	0 51	1 1	1 11	1 20	1 30	1 40	1 50	10
11	0 2	0 12	0 22	0 31	0 41	0 51	1 1	1 11	1 21	1 31	1 40	1 50	11
12	0 2	0 12	0 22	0 32	0 41	0 51	1 1	1 11	1 21	1 31	1 41	1 50	12
13	0 2	0 12	0 22	0 32	0 42	0 51	1 1	1 11	1 21	1 31	1 41	1 51	13
14	0 2	0 12	0 22	0 32	0 42	0 52	1 1	1 11	1 21	1 31	1 41	1 51	14
15	0 2	0 12	0 22	0 32	0 42	0 52	1 2	1 11	1 21	1 31	1 41	1 51	15
16	0 3	0 12	0 22	0 32	0 42	0 52	1 2	1 12	1 21	1 31	1 41	1 51	16
17	0 3	0 13	0 23	0 32	0 42	0 52	1 2	1 12	1 22	1 32	1 41	1 51	17
18	0 3	0 13	0 23	0 33	0 42	0 52	1 2	1 12	1 22	1 32	1 42	1 51	18
19	0 3	0 13	0 23	0 33	0 43	0 52	1 2	1 12	1 22	1 32	1 42	1 52	19
20	0 3	0 13	0 23	0 33	0 43	0 53	1 2	1 12	1 22	1 32	1 42	1 52	20
21	0 3	0 13	0 23	0 33	0 43	0 53	1 3	1 12	1 22	1 32	1 42	1 52	21
22	0 4	0 13	0 23	0 33	0 43	0 53	1 3	1 13	1 22	1 32	1 42	1 52	22
23	0 4	0 14	0 23	0 33	0 43	0 53	1 3	1 13	1 23	1 32	1 42	1 52	23
24	0 4	0 14	0 24	0 34	0 43	0 53	1 3	1 13	1 23	1 33	1 43	1 52	24
25	0 4	0 14	0 24	0 34	0 44	0 53	1 3	1 13	1 23	1 33	1 43	1 53	25
26	0 4	0 14	0 24	0 34	0 44	0 54	1 3	1 13	1 23	1 33	1 43	1 53	26
27	0 4	0 14	0 24	0 34	0 44	0 54	1 4	1 13	1 23	1 33	1 43	1 53	27
28	0 5	0 14	0 24	0 34	0 44	0 54	1 4	1 14	1 23	1 33	1 43	1 53	28
29	0 5	0 15	0 24	0 34	0 44	0 54	1 4	1 14	1 24	1 33	1 43	1 53	29
30	0 5	0 15	0 25	0 34	0 44	0 54	1 4	1 14	1 24	1 34	1 43	1 53	30
31	0 5	0 15	0 25	0 35	0 45	0 54	1 4	1 14	1 24	1 34	1 44	1 54	31
32	0 5	0 15	0 25	0 35	0 45	0 55	1 4	1 14	1 24	1 34	1 44	1 54	32
33	0 5	0 15	0 25	0 35	0 45	0 55	1 5	1 14	1 24	1 34	1 44	1 54	33
34	0 6	0 15	0 25	0 35	0 45	0 55	1 5	1 15	1 24	1 34	1 44	1 54	34
35	0 6	0 16	0 25	0 35	0 45	0 55	1 5	1 15	1 25	1 34	1 44	1 54	35
36	0 6	0 16	0 26	0 35	0 45	0 55	1 5	1 15	1 25	1 35	1 44	1 54	36
37	0 6	0 16	0 26	0 36	0 46	0 55	1 5	1 15	1 25	1 35	1 45	1 54	37
38	0 6	0 16	0 26	0 36	0 46	0 56	1 5	1 15	1 25	1 35	1 45	1 55	38
39	0 6	0 16	0 26	0 36	0 46	0 56	1 6	1 15	1 25	1 35	1 45	1 55	39
40	0 7	0 16	0 26	0 36	0 46	0 56	1 6	1 16	1 25	1 35	1 45	1 55	40
41	0 7	0 17	0 26	0 36	0 46	0 56	1 6	1 16	1 26	1 35	1 45	1 55	41
42	0 7	0 17	0 27	0 36	0 46	0 56	1 6	1 16	1 26	1 36	1 45	1 55	42
43	0 7	0 17	0 27	0 37	0 46	0 56	1 6	1 16	1 26	1 36	1 46	1 55	43
44	0 7	0 17	0 27	0 37	0 47	0 57	1 6	1 16	1 26	1 36	1 46	1 56	44
45	0 7	0 17	0 27	0 37	0 47	0 57	1 7	1 16	1 26	1 36	1 46	1 56	45
46	0 8	0 17	0 27	0 37	0 47	0 57	1 7	1 17	1 26	1 36	1 46	1 56	46
47	0 8	0 18	0 27	0 37	0 47	0 57	1 7	1 17	1 27	1 36	1 46	1 56	47
48	0 8	0 18	0 28	0 37	0 47	0 57	1 7	1 17	1 27	1 37	1 46	1 56	48
49	0 8	0 18	0 28	0 38	0 47	0 57	1 7	1 17	1 27	1 37	1 47	1 56	49
50	0 8	0 18	0 28	0 38	0 48	0 57	1 7	1 17	1 27	1 37	1 47	1 57	50
51	0 8	0 18	0 28	0 38	0 48	0 58	1 8	1 17	1 27	1 37	1 47	1 57	51
52	0 9	0 18	0 28	0 38	0 48	0 58	1 8	1 18	1 27	1 37	1 47	1 57	52
53	0 9	0 19	0 28	0 38	0 48	0 58	1 8	1 18	1 28	1 37	1 47	1 57	53
54	0 9	0 19	0 29	0 38	0 48	0 58	1 8	1 18	1 28	1 38	1 47	1 57	54
55	0 9	0 19	0 29	0 39	0 48	0 58	1 8	1 18	1 28	1 38	1 48	1 57	55
56	0 9	0 19	0 29	0 39	0 49	0 58	1 8	1 18	1 28	1 38	1 48	1 58	56
57	0 9	0 19	0 29	0 39	0 49	0 59	1 8	1 19	1 28	1 38	1 48	1 58	57
58	0 10	0 19	0 29	0 39	0 49	0 59	1 9	1 19	1 28	1 38	1 48	1 58	58
59	0 10	0 20	0 29	0 39	0 49	0 59	1 9	1 19	1 29	1 38	1 48	1 58	59
60	0 10	0 20	0 30	0 39	0 49	0 59	1 9	1 19	1 29	1 39	1 48	1 58	60

Index

The figures in *italics* indicate a line drawing or chart.

Acceleration, 10
Angles, 111
Angular, 19, 111, *125*
Arabic Parts, 108
Ascendant, 11, 12, 18, 22, 26, 26, 106-7, 111
Aspect grid, *10*, 19
Aspects, calculation of, 32-4; major, 30-1, 74-82, 82-9, 89-97, 97-104; minor, 31-2; patterns, 114
Asteriods, 110

Birth chart, 8, 9-19, *10*, 112-14, *113*
British Summer Time, 21, *125-6*

Cadent, 19, 111, *125*
Cardinal, 111
Cusp, 12, 26

Date changes, 21
Daylight Saving Time, 20, *126*
Descendant, 111
Detriment, 19, 106
Direct, 110

Elements, 18, 105
Ephemerides, 7, 9, *121-2*
Exaltation, 19, 106

Fall, 19, 106
Fixed, 111

GMT, 11, 20, 125-6

Hemisphere, 22-3, *24*, 110, 112
House divisions, 9, 12, 19, 23, 25, *125*
Houses, 25-29, 110, 55-73, *123-4*

Jupiter, 16, 45-7, 64-6, 79, 87, 94-5, 102-3

Longtitude equivalent, 22
Longtitudes, 9, 11, *120*

Mars, 16, 43-5, 62-4, 78-9, 86-7, 94, 101-2

Mercury, 15, 39-41, 59-60, 76-7, 84-5, 92, 99-100
Midheaven, 13, 107-8, 111
Midpoints, 109
Moon, 7, 9, 14, 29, 38-9, 57-8, 75-6, 83-4, 90-91, 98-9, 109

Neptune, 17, 51-2, 70-2, 88-9, 96-7, 104

Planets, 7, 9, 55-73, 74-105; motion, 9; positions, 13; retrograde, 110; rising, 18, 106-7; ruling, 18
Planetary Emphasis, 110-111; dignities, 106, *119*
Pluto, 17, 53-4, 72-3, 89, 97, 104
Progressions, 118
Ptolemy, 23

Quadruplicities, 18
Quadrants, 110, 111-12

Rulership, 7, 106
Rising sign *see* ascendant

Saturn, 17, 47-9, 66-8, 87-8, 95-6, 103
Siderial time, 9, 11, 12, 21-2; correction *127*
Stars, fixed, 109
Succedent, 19, 111, *125*
Sun, 7, 13, 29, 35-8, 55-7, 74, 82-3, 89-90, 97-8

Time zones, 21
Transits, 118
Triplicities, 18

Uranus, 17, 49-50, 68-70, 88, 96, 104

Venus, 15, 41-3, 60-2, 78, 85-6, 93, 100-1

Zodiac signs, *6*, 7, 35-54; classification, 105-6
Zone standard, 10